Notre Dame, We Hail Thee- Your Influence on a Life

John Fremont Fisher

Table of Contents

FOREWORD

John Fisher wasn't just a roommate in medical school, he is in large part of why I graduated. No, it was not that he inspired me, though he did, it was because I was dyslexic and couldn't comprehend and take notes at the same time. I borrowed John's notes and transcribed them so I had a comprehensible version of the days' lectures. As copying lecture notes saved me, so too has reading about *the innocent minds of children* rescued me from the rigidness of my adult ways. As John writes in God, Atheism, and Becoming Like Little Children, "What is it that little kids have that we have left behind?" "… we will all hopefully have time for our own search for childlike innocence."

Just as St. Teresa of Calcutta (Mother Teresa) had her epic struggles with doubts in the existence of God, we too are allowed to have our doubts. Inspirational, courageous, and authentic, John helps us with an approach to faith; "If you are out there, Lord, please help my unbelief. A Loving Creator would not likely say, "No" to his creatures for such a humble request before death." (God, Atheism, and Becoming Like Little Children).

I support and share the concepts as detailed in "The Phone and I." The phone is truly a distraction that has deprived us of time with ourselves. John captures this best with; "I will relish the silence of quiet contemplation about my time on this planet with family, friends, and former patients, grateful that I am still alive, hoping that I have made a difference to some of these people. I might even pray."

While today's academics chart a dangerous secular path, John's writings are a steadfast reminder of our fundamental values and faith in God. Once again, John sends a lifeline, to a renewed spirit of faith in God, to me and to all who read and reflect on the essays that follow.

Pat Finelli, M.D.

Clinical Professor of Neurology

Hartford Hospital, Hartford, CT

Acknowledgements

This book would not have been possible without the support of my sweet wife of 47 years, Peggy Fisher, who encouraged me to compile my writings in one place. Our six children, three girls (twins Audrey Elizabeth and Brigid, and Mary Kate) and three boys (Brendan, Stewart, and Luke—all rabid ND fans-- always gave me favorable feedback for my essays they read whether I really deserved it or not. I continue to be inspired by my love for our 16 grandchildren— so fortunate to be their "Granddad."

My cousin Robert Macdonald, son of my mother's beloved sister Ruth, was on campus at Notre Dame during my years there. A year ahead of me, he never held back important critical comments I needed both then and now. He sent me the above photo of the Golden Dome at night along with an array of Track Changes to my Introduction. His oldest brother John, another Domer, enthusiastically supported me in this endeavor.

Dick Leonhardt ("Steamer"), my lifelong friend from the Notre Dame Glee Club, could always be bring his great bass voice to our formal concerts as well as informal singing of our favorites anywhere--even in the stairwells if necessary. He sent me the photo which appears on the cover and the photo of the Golden Dome in winter.

My medical school roommate, Pasquale (Pat) Finelli has probably read most of the contents of this book over the years and was always my advocate. If he felt (rightly) that I was definitely no wordsmith, he never said so and he was kind enough to write the Foreward.

I certainly wish to thank *Notre Dame Magazine*, and editors, Kerry Temple and John Nagy, for publishing "A Doctor's Prescription" and for my tribute to the Glee Club and to our beloved director, Daniel H. Pedtke ("Remembering the Glee Club's 'Dean' Pedtke"). He and my Glee Club buddies have made all the difference in my life.

I am also indebted to John Paul Meenan, editor of *Catholic Insight Magazine* for allowing me to re-publish so many of my religious reflections.

Most importantly, I want to acknowledge the University of Notre Dame and the late Father John Cavanaugh, former president of the University and my senior professor of theology, for grounding me in my Catholic faith, which remains very much a work in progress.

John Fremont Fisher MD

Augusta, Georgia September

26, 2023

INTRODUCTION

I am a passionately proud alumnus of the University of Notre Dame from the Class of 1965. The seed to someday call myself an ND student was planted in a vague childhood memory of my Uncle Ray taking me to see the Fighting Irish play the USC Trojans in the Los Angeles Coliseum in 1953 when my family lived in Manhattan Beach, California. During my teenage years in Grosse Ile, Michigan, I spent several vacations with my cousins in Pittsburgh, the Macdonalds and the Kilkearys. Bob Macdonald, a pediatrician and my role model in becoming a physician, and Joe Kilkeary, a hotel manager, were married to two of my mother's sisters. Bob's oldest son, John, was then a student at Notre Dame, and two of Joe's sons were there with John. John's brothers, Rob and Jay, similarly influenced, were there in my time. On holidays, I listened mesmerized to all my cousins' tales about the school with boyish admiration, and no other college was ever even on my radar. I had to go there.

I applied to Notre Dame in my senior year at St. Patrick's High School. It was most likely a "close play at home plate," but the "umpires" on the Notre Dame Admissions Committee called me "safe" and Notre Dame decided to take a flier on me. I remember being tearful leaving home for the last time on that September day in 1961 when freshmen were due to arrive on campus.

Except for the Friday pep rallies and Saturday game days, my first few months as a student were memorable, but could have been more pleasant. Pre-med studies were difficult (pink slips at mid- semester in a couple of subjects). Some of my roommates in 343 Farley Hall and a few others on the third floor seemed to resent my studying in the library and not back in the dorm horsing around with them. They found it amusing to play imaginative practical jokes at my expense on several occasions.

Not surprisingly, I opted for a single room in Lyons Hall as a sophomore. One football Saturday, a member of the Glee Club heard me strumming on my guitar and singing a Kingston Trio number and suggested that I try out for the Club. My successful audition the following week changed my entire life. Because I was placed with the second tenors and tenors are scarce in any glee club, I soon qualified to travel to off-campus concerts and weekend trips in the surrounding states. Most Glee Clubbers were regular guys who could sing and carry a tune, but they became my "fraternity brothers" at a university without fraternities. Many have remained my cherished friends for life.

Our gentle, organ virtuoso of a director, Daniel Pedkte (the Dean), was a modest, genuinely holy man who brought out our best in four-part harmony in classical choral works, Irish ballads, lullabies, Broadway tunes, and college songs. Our rendition of the famous Notre Dame Victory March always brought our audiences to their feet and even gave *us* chill bumps. We never seemed to tire of several of our favorites, one of which Dean wrote himself before my time during a copyrighter's strike when copyrighted music couldn't be sung. The words to the song are about Notre Dame (Our Lady):

Notre Dame, we hail thee

Mother, fond and true

Heaven's beauties veil thee

With thy gold and blue

Through life's deepening shadows Or in

glory's flame

Grateful sons shall love and praise thee, Notre Dame

I have to believe that she has been listening-in every time that song has been sung and has used her motherly influence to point all of us and anyone with even a remote connection to Our Lady's school in the direction of her Son. Despite the countless times I have disappointed them, I now see why I was accepted as a student there—to point *me* in His direction. Her spirit is very much alive on that campus in so many different ways: in philosophy and theology courses, with daily Mass in dorm chapels, retreats, campus ministries and outreach there and abroad, and yes, even in ND football games. I must add that I'm not sure what her take would be on "Hail Mary" passes in the end zone at the end of a game, but it *is* her school. Some haven't recognized her presence in their youthful naivete. I didn't see it until my senior-year, theology course taught by a former president of the University, Father John Cavanaugh. Looking back six decades, it has become oh so clear! Virtually all my non-scientific writings reflect my hidden agenda for this book, whether they are about my philosophy of medicine, religious views, music, and even humor—to point myself, my family, and others who might read some of these pages to Our Blessed Lord. Thank you, Notre Dame. May God forgive me for the times I've wasted.

College Years

Lost at Notre Dame Without a Song and Without 'The Dean'

John Fremont Fisher, MD (Notre Dame '65) *

*Published in part in *Notre Dame Magazine* as, "Remembering the Glee Club's "Dean" Pedtke May 24, 2016

My uncle drove me to campus and helped me take my belongings to the third floor of Farley Hall that muggy September afternoon of 1961. Dad was in the hospital recovering from his appendectomy the night before. With uneasy anticipation, I entered Room 343 and rather awkwardly introduced myself and Uncle Fremont to my assigned new roommates, Howie and Chuck. They were nice enough, but rather non-descript teenagers like myself. I hope I remembered to thank Uncle "Freem" before he left, but I immediately began less-than-compulsively stowing my stuff and then loitering in the hallway with the other new freshmen of our wing, all of us now officially connected to Knute Rockne, the Four Horsemen, Frank Leahy, Johnny Lujack, Angelo Bertelli, and Paul Hornung.

Once classes began in earnest, some of these lads like my roommate, Chuck, continued to loiter ubiquitously anywhere, but now attired in new ND sweatshirts from the bookstore. Alarmed by what might befall me in the form of exams, I could be found until 10:45ish (curfew was at 11:00PM for freshmen) Sunday through Thursday in the library for the first week or two. Easily distracted by rustling papers and hoarse whispers amid those crowded tables, I searched for and "holed-up" in silent hideouts like basement storage rooms and even back stairwells. Unless a Monday quiz loomed, I had been imprinted since childhood against studying on Friday nights and the tumult and the shouting at the Field House pulled me to the pep rally like a magnet. After some raucous cheering with each rabble- rousing speech and witnessing the teetering and collapse of several human pyramids, it was out to the Circle for a bus ride to the Philadelphia restaurant where there was at least the remote hope of meeting a cute waitress, a St. Mary's girl, or running into a DHQ* downtown. Unfortunately, this 'wild goose chase' never bagged any birds and most of the conversation was *about* rather than *to* girls. 1

On Saturdays the entire campus always effervesced with game-day excitement even though the glory days of ND football had long gone. Owing to the tremendous popularity of the Kingston Trio and folk music in my era, there seemed to be guitarist on every dorm portico fighting the constant feedback from a jerry-rigged sound system and anxious to entertain. Armed with a shrill voice and three chords, these troubadours were hoping to attract the notice of someone's cute, starry-eyed sister passing by. Undoubtedly buoyed by the undiscerning past praises of their families, they were completely unaware that the guitars were as out-of-tune as their voices. Small wonder that their performances failed to attract any serious feminine attention.

Nevertheless, crowd watching was in and studying was out on Saturdays too. By 1:00PM, most of us had followed the band and at least five choruses of the *Victory March* into the stadium full of anticipation and hope. The Irish went five and five in the Fall of 1961 and we lost to Ara Parseghian's pesky Northwestern team for the third time in a row. So, there was little to cheer about except that we beat Southern Cal and our in-state rival, Purdue. However, the undisputed highlight of that season was the winning field goal with no time on the clock kicked by Joe Perkowski despite the heroics of Syracuse's redoubtable Ernie Davis. As time ran out with Notre Dame trailing 14-15, Joe's first attempt from 56 yards failed, but officials gave him another try from 15 yards closer for 'roughing the kicker'. The controversial, second kick through the uprights was followed by

------

1 *'Dining Hall Queen'—a girl our age, younger, or older, who was employed in the dining hall.

joyous pandemonium in the stadium and all evening in the dorms and downtown.

Notre Dame football, the Grotto, and Mass at the Basilica were the only antidotes for the bleak fall and winter of my freshman year. Despite my version of hard studying, I received pink slips in three of my five subjects after mid-terms. Returning to Farley after redoubling my efforts at learning in the evenings, I found 343 had become the designated rumpus room for at least seven of my hall mates with Howie and Chuck holding court. Consequently, sleep in the upper berth of my bunk between 11:00 and 12:00 midnight was generally out of the question. If I did happen to doze off in the din, I might be awakened by my own imminent or actual urinary incontinence discovering my hand had been immersed in a container of warm water amid the guffaws of several juvenile 18-year-olds. Homesickness had set in with a vengeance.

Howie was bright and did well without seeming effort, I surprised myself with decent grades, but the hapless Chuck was sent home packing after finals. He had a lot of laughs while amassing a GPA of less than 1.0. I often wondered what his parents thought and whether he still wore any ND paraphernalia. Howie and I were moved to the four-man room across the hall to join Nick and Art where there were two vacancies probably because of a fate similar to that of Chuck.

Nick was super-smart and a good guy, but one night when I came home early and was already in bed, I overheard Art enter the room and begin telling the other two how much he liked to play pranks on me. He apparently resented my nightly study outside the dorm. He referred to his unkind 'jokes' as "forcefully disassembling my testicular tissue"—only he used other words. He only laughed sardonically when I announced my presence from my bunk behind the lockers. The pranks became so frequent that I began a nightly, post-study ritual which included feeling in my lower bunk for short- sheeting and tacks in the bed. On one occasion I came back to the dorm room and went through my usual bunk-bed "liturgy" and found nothing out of the ordinary. Shortly after getting into bed, I became aware of running footsteps and someone leaping onto the upper bunk. As planned, the landing then drenched me with a cupful of water which was dislodged, hidden in the bedsprings overhead. What rollicking fun for all!

One fateful night, so as not to disturb my entire floor, let alone incur the wrath of my friend, Art, I was typing a paper at 3:00AM in a basement room barely big enough for a table and chair. I should have suspected he was awake and planning another fiendish caper with the guy down the hall. Suddenly, the door to my little cell burst open with great force and at easily 100 decibels and in rushed a figure dressed in black. His face was disguised with green shaving cream. He had a lit candle in one hand and was brandishing a butcher knife with the other which he feigned to direct at my heart. All I could do in my startled state of alarm was to scream aloud. I had no idea such blood-curdling volume was in me. This was followed by the fitful laughing of the perpetrator, Art, and several others in on the event as they ran down the hall.

There were other tricks too hilarious to recount. Nick excelled in his studies and was admitted to the Blue Circle, Howie continued to flourish, and Art was mercifully returned to his home in Tenafly, NJ, by the Administration at the end of the semester. Nick and Howie often laughed at, but were not complicit in Art's practical jokes, but neither were they true-blue friends who came to my defense and I had had enough of roommates. Accordingly, I arranged for a single room in the basement of Lyons Hall for sophomore year.

Now in pre-med, studying for Emil T's[2] and Brother Raphael's[3] exams amidst the dorm cacophony was still not conducive to good grades; so it was back to the stairwells for me.

One football Saturday, Bob Koches, a member of the Notre Dame Glee Club, heard me strumming my guitar and singing one of the Kingston Trio's songs and suggested that I should try out for the Glee Club.

Determined to achieve the GPA which would not cause medical school admission committees to stifle a laugh, I had not considered joining anything extracurricular, let alone the Glee Club whose members I erroneously assumed were all music majors. Nevertheless, I acted on Bob's suggestion and he took me over to the rehearsal hall to meet Professor Daniel H. Pedtke, affectionately known by the lads as 'The Dean.' Within minutes, Dean was playing scales on the piano for me to imitate and with an approving nod and a gentle "yeah" he told me to sit with the second tenors when rehearsal began momentarily at 5:00PM. I knew none of the songs, but when 90-plus men's voices broke out with the *Victory March* a cappella in four-part harmony, I was suddenly all chill bumps and hooked for life. The memories of freshman year and all the laughs at my expense evaporated. The Glee Club became my fraternity on a campus where they were not allowed.

Rehearsing every weekday afternoon from 5:00 to 6:00PM became part of my very fiber for the rest of my time at Notre Dame. After rehearsals, once I had learned my part on a few songs, I became a nightly annoyance to some of the veteran Clubbers, boyishly bugging them to sing some more as several of us walked from O'Shaughnessy to the Dining Hall. I could never be accused of having an operatic voice, but the Good Lord did allow me to have reasonably good pitch and volume. Indeed, in my enthusiasm for four-part harmony, I often erred on the side of being too loud rather than blending. Dean taught me to have a better feel for a song and back off some when appropriate, but I deserved the mostly affectionate reputation I got of being a 'screamer'. Like most young men who can

---

2 Emil T. Hoffman, PhD, Professor of Chemistry (much feared, iconic figure whose course weeded out many pre-meds and re-directed many careers.)

3 Brother Raphael Wilson, C.S.C., PhD, Professor of Biology and later Director of Admissions (He gave me a rude awakening after I failed his first exam. He was also benevolent and understanding in allowing me to take an exam for which I overslept after an all-nighter of studying.)

carry a tune, many of the friends I made in the Club were baritones with good voices, but the Indiana Motor Bus Company's buses held only 40—39 singers and Dean. Baritones were plentiful; tenors were not. Consequently, through no great talent of mine, I was soon one of the 39 regulars on off-campus concerts and in these travels made the closest friends of my life. Some still are. One in particular was a first tenor. He and I became like brothers. I doubt if there are many who can claim a 'best friend of all time' whose name is exactly the same, spelled exactly the same way, John Fisher. He became Fish I and I became Fish II. At John's wedding (yes, I was Best Man too), the officiating priest who gave the homily quipped that he hoped he would remember which John Fisher should recite the vows. I've never been prouder to be a Best Man.

Dean Pedtke was a one-of-a-kind choral director who, with his back to the audience, could say so much to us on the risers with just his hands and facial expression. There was no grandiose, wild waving of both arms in time. He kept the all-important rhythm with his hands in front of his chest mostly concealed from the patrons. With just his fingertips, he communicated the starts and stops in a piece without any confusion and with a simple rotation of his hands, the louds and softs in a song or hymn which can move an audience to tears or exhilaration. And in that face, not handsome but careworn, were the most expressive eyes I've ever known. We were mesmerized into knowing exactly what kind of a sound he wanted us to produce, soft and tender or full-throated and boisterous. Although we knew intuitively what to do, at times stage-fright, sagging pitch, fatigue, or simply trying too hard prevented some of the chords from locking. We could tell from Dean's countenance at the end of a number whether he was pleased with our performance of it. A neutral expression to us followed by a perfunctory turn to the audience to accept the applause indicated that our interpretation of the song had been adequate. But, if Dean paused for a moment after the final chord and gave us a fatherly nod and a wink before turning around, we knew we had "nailed it" and the vigor in the clapping which followed from something deeply experienced by the crowd was palpable. Dean's unassuming visage and dress and gentle nature could never be described as charismatic, but the sheer depth of his character, personal goodness, and his credentials as a musician made an indelible mark on each of us. Every time he stepped up to conduct us, our entire focus was to please this man whom we loved.

We were all unified in our admiration for Dean. Our audiences could have chosen the Norman Luboff Choir or the Robert Shaw Chorale for technically better performances, but some connection to Notre Dame put them in the seats. To them we personified, their own or a relative's alma mater, Knute Rockne and Notre Dame football, or perhaps just their pride in being a Catholic. And Dean could always make them glad they came with his special interpretation and mix of classical pieces, famous songs from yesteryear, show tunes, and comedy trios and quartets. When we sensed on the risers that a performance was going well, we couldn't wait to get to the college songs finale which everyone expected from us because we knew they would jump to their feet immediately when they heard Dean make that *Victory March* ring. It is simply the gold standard and no other fight song is so universally recognized or loved.

There was a group of us whose affection for the Glee Club was on a different level altogether. It had to do with the fervor each of us had for singing, for Notre Dame, and for the unassuming, genuinely decent man who seemed to be able to take fairly average voices to unexpected heights in harmony on stages all across America. Hero worship would be close to the mark to depict our love for Dean except that he was far from handsome or dashing. He wouldn't light up any room he entered unless we happened to be there. We often smiled affectionately at his use of 1940s exclamationslike "Gee" and "Golly" in casual conversation. We thought Dean was "cool." The majority of Clubbers didn't notice. Their appreciation of Dean was as a music director. We pejoratively referred to them as the "A Group." We were the "B Group." That stratification had a history before my time extending back to an overnight, off-campus concert where there were two hotels needed because of a room shortage, one rather plush and the other rather not. Some members rushed to be at the head of the line for the better hotel. The rest had to settle for the other. The former were forever referred to as the "A Group."

Through the years each group took on a certain distinctive personality. The "A Group" were of the early-to-bed, buttoned-up sort. "B Groupers" were up late after concerts scouring the host city for a quiet bar in which to keep harmonizing even if the quality had become suspect after a few beers and without Dean. With the right mix of voice parts, a bunch of ordinary looking college guys could stun the patrons and bartender of a tavern by breaking into a four-part rendition of the *Victory March*. After that debut and a few of our favorite songs, we never bought another beer and left many half-empty, "dead soldiers" on the bar. If there were no bars nearby, a six- pack and a motel stairwell would do quite nicely for a post-concert "scream." Two o'clock AM was the usual time for us "B Groupers" to put a sock in it, but all of us were tied together by Dean and the songs in our hearts.

The rest of my Notre Dame years sped by with the Glee Club actually facilitating my pre-med studies by giving me an outlet to unclutter my mind once in a while. Dean made use of my rather strident voice and "hamminess" by featuring me in some comedic songs and Gilbert and Sullivan's *Trial by Jury*. My only heartbreak came in my failed run for Glee Club President. I was defeated in a landslide by one of my friends who had the easy demeanor of Andy Griffith in his visits with potential Glee Club voters, while I was overly scripted and too earnest in my campaign appeal and more like Barney Fife. The Glee Club had come to mean so very much to me, I couldn't help it. After the election results came in, I walked dejectedly to a remote spot on the golf course and cried my eyes out. Our thoughtful student director sensed my disappointment and tracked me down out there and I'll never forget his kind gesture of understanding and comfort. I hope at the post-election party that night I made a "good fist of it" in being gracious in defeat.

There is no question in my mind that being a member of the Glee Club gave my life at Notre Dame real meaning and I actually believe helped me get into medical school. However, from 5:00 to 6:00 PM weekdays, now a medical student in Richmond, VA, I was so used to singing choral music, I felt somewhat lost. So, I started my own glee club at the Medical College of Virginia and on the appointed day about 40 showed up to join—all women. There was nothing else to do but conduct the group which I did until I had to learn at the bedside with patients two years later.

Dean's influence on me has continued for the better part of fifty years and led me to singing in the Naval Air Training Command Choir in Pensacola, FL in my years as a Navy Flight Surgeon, fifteen years in a barbershop quartet, and to directing the barbershop chorus for seven. Though the years keep diminishing our numbers, 10-20 of us hard-core "B groupers" from the '60s still meet somewhere every year in a mini-reunion and sing ourselves hoarse for our wives and families before and after a ND football game. Some of our harmonies don't seem half-bad to us, but if Dean is listening and wincing is allowed in Heaven, I'm sure has done it or at least said, "Gee." After all, the "geezer factor" in our group is getting stronger and stronger. Although my formal choral music days are behind me, I've come full circle and have been playing guitar and singing Irish songs in a bar every Tuesday evening for more than 20 years.

As a fortunate spin-off of all this performing, I believe it has made me unafraid in front of an audience and a decent medical educator--my real vocation. My sweet wife and six children know how much singing defines me and have tolerated this "disorder" of mine very patiently over the years. As I gaze at a photograph I have in my office of Daniel H. Pedtke conducting the Notre Dame Glee Club, I hope he would be mostly—but not all—proud of his not-so- very-talented protégé. I hope I have brought at least some joy into the hearts of anyone who has deigned to listen to me, but I can't hold a candle to the saintly man who thrilled so many for 35 years. Despite

an inauspicious start, Dean Pedtke helped me find my real Notre Dame.
God bless them both.

Surviving Freshman Year at Notre Dame (Did I Really Want to Become a Doctor That Bad?) or How Singing Saved My Immortal Soul.

John F. Fisher, MD (ND'65)

Without a clue to the life of a physician, for several years I had been proclaiming to my teachers and buddies at St. Patrick's High School, and to both sides of my family that I was going to become a doctor and go to Notre Dame. On my Irish Catholic mother's side, we were an ND family. A favorite uncle, my inspiration as a physician, and three of his sons were Domers. So, loaded down with luggage and a guitar case, my uncle Fremont and I climbed the stairs to the third floor of Farley Hall that sweltering afternoon of September, 1961, the day incoming freshmen were to arrive on campus. Dad was in a hospital bed recovering from his appendectomy the night before, or he would have come. Dyspneic and sweating with uneasy anticipation, I entered Room 343 and rather awkwardly introduced myself to my assigned new roommates, Howie and Chuck, both friendly, but rather nondescript teenagers like myself. I hope I remembered to thank Uncle "Freem" before he left, but I immediately began less-than-compulsively stowing my stuff and then loitering in the hallway with the other new freshmen of our wing, all of us now officially connected to Knute Rockne, George Gipp, the Four Horsemen, Frank Leahy, Johnny Lujack, Angelo Bertelli, and Paul Hornung. Once classes began in earnest, some of these lads like my roommate, Chuck, continued to loiter ubiquitously anywhere, but now proudly clad in new ND sweatshirts from the bookstore.

Perhaps skeptical from my SAT scores about my aptitude for a career in medicine, the Admission's Committee hadn't accepted me into the school's Science Pre-Med program, but indicated that I might qualify for A.B. Pre-Med with decent grades by sophomore year. Thus incentivized, but alarmed by the inevitability of difficult exams, I could be found until 10:45ish (curfew was at 11:00PM for freshmen) Sunday through Thursday in the library for the first week or two. Crowded tables, rustling papers, and hoarse whispers amid the dank air which hinted of teenage body odor soon drove me to the haunting stillness of basement storage rooms and even back stairwells. Unless a Monday quiz loomed, I had been imprinted since childhood against studying on Friday nights and the tumult and the shouting at the Field House drew me to the pep rally like a zombie. After some raucous cheering with each rabble-rousing speech and witnessing the teetering and collapse of several human pyramids, it was out to the Circle for a bus ride to the Philadelphia restaurant where there was at least the remote hope of meeting a cute waitress, a St. Mary's girl, or running into a Dining Hall Queen downtown. Unfortunately, this 'wild goose chase' neverbaggedanybirds andmost of the conversation was *about* rather than *to* girls.

On Saturdays, the entire campus always effervesced with game-day excitement even though the glory days of ND football had long gone. Owing to the tremendous popularity of the Kingston Trio and folk music in my era, there seemed to be a guitarist on every dorm portico unfazed by the constant feedback from a jerry-rigged sound system and eager to entertain. Armed with a shrill voice and three chords, these troubadours were hoping to attract the notice of someone's cute, starry-eyed sister passing by. Undoubtedly buoyed by the undiscerning past praises of their families, they were completely unaware that the guitars were as out-of-tune as their voices. Small wonder that their performances failed to attract any serious feminine attention. Nevertheless, crowd watching was *in* and my pre-med studying was *out* on Saturdays too. By 1:00PM, most of us had followed the band and at least five choruses of the *Victory March* into the stadium full of anticipation and hope.

Notre Dame football, the Grotto, and Mass at the Basilica were the only antidotes for the bleak fall and winter of my freshman year.

Despite *my* version of hard studying, I received pink slips in three of my five subjects after mid-terms and I could sense that my career in medicine was ebbing away. Returning to Farley after redoubling my efforts at learning in the evenings, I found 343 had become the designated smoking lounge for at least seven of my hall mates with Howie and Chuck holding court. Consequently, sleep in the upper berth of my bunk between 11:00 and 12:00 midnight was nigh impossible. If I did happen to doze off in the din, I might be awakened by a severe urge to void finding my hand immersed in a container of warm water amid the guffaws of several juvenile 18-year-olds. Homesickness had set in with a vengeance.

Howie was bright and did well without seeming effort, I surprised myself with decent first-semester grades, but the hapless Chuck was sent home packing after finals. He had a lot of laughs while amassing a GPA of less than 1.0. Howie and I were moved to the four-man room across the hall to join Nick and Art where there were two vacancies probably because of a fate similar to that of Chuck.

Nick was super-smart and a good guy, but one night when I came home early and was already in bed, I overheard Art enter the room and begin telling the other two how much he liked to play pranks on me. He apparently resented my nightly study outside the dorm. He referred to his unkind 'jokes' as "forcefully disassembling my testicular tissue"—only he used other words. He only laughed sardonically when I made him aware of my presence from my bunk behind the lockers. The pranks became so frequent that I began a nightly post-study ritual which included feeling in my lower bunk for short-sheeting and tacks in the bed. On one occasion I came back to the dorm room and went through my usual bunk-bed "liturgy" and found nothing out of the ordinary. Shortly after getting into bed, however, I became aware of running footsteps and someone leaping onto the upper bunk. As planned, the landing then drenched me with a cupful of water which was dislodged, hidden in the bedsprings overhead. What rollicking fun for all!

One fateful night, so as not to disturb my entire floor, let alone incur the wrath of my friend, Art, I was typing a paper at 3:00AM in a basement room barely big enough for a table and chair. I should have suspected he was awake and planning another fiendish caper with the guy down the hall. Suddenly, the door to my little cell burst open with great force at easily 100 decibels and in stormed a figure dressed in black. His face was disguised with green shaving cream. He had a lit candle in one hand and was brandishing a butcher knife with the other which he feigned to direct at my heart. All I could do in my startled state of alarm was to scream aloud. I had no idea I such blood-curdling volume was in me. This was followed by the fitful laughing of the perpetrator, Art, and several others in on the event as they ran down the hall.

There were other tricks too hilarious to recount. Nick excelled in his studies and was admitted to the Blue Circle, Howie continued to flourish, and Art was mercifully returned to his home in Tenafly, NJ, by the Administration at the end of the semester. Nick and Howie often laughed at, but were not complicit in Art's practical jokes, but neither were they true-blue friends who came to my defense and I had had enough of roommates. Accordingly, I arranged for a single room in the basement of Lyons Hall for sophomore year more determined than ever to become a physician.

Now in A.B Pre-med, studying for Emil T's [Hoffman, PHD Chemistry] and Brother Raphael's [Wilson, Biology] exams amidst the dorm cacophony was still not conducive to good grades; so it was back to the stairwells for me. One football Saturday, Bob Koches, a member of the Notre Dame Glee Club, heard me strumming my guitar and singing a Kingston Trio song. Either he had had a rough Friday night or his credentials as a music critic were bogus. Nevertheless, he suggested that I should audition for the Glee Club before the next 5:00 PM rehearsal.

Determined to achieve the GPA which would not cause medical school admission committees to stifle a laugh, I had not

considered joining anything extracurricular, let alone the Glee Club whose members I erroneously assumed were all music majors. They were not as I proved 'in spades' to the beloved Director, "The Dean"-
-Professor Daniel H. Pedtke, in my audition. Dean took a flier on me and put me with the second tenors during the rehearsal. When 90-plus men's voices broke out with the *Victory March a cappella* in four- part harmony, I was suddenly all chill bumps and hooked for life. The memories of freshman year and all the laughs at my expense evaporated. The Glee Club became my fraternity on a campus where they were not allowed and gave me some of the best friends of my life. Sharing their love of singing and harmony and learning my second-tenor part of the traveling repertoire gave me, for the first time, a sense that I truly belonged at this school. My green Notre Dame Glee Club blazer and performance white tie and tails became *my* 'Fighting Irish' uniforms. Donning them and breaking into song evoked deep nostalgia for whatever Notre Dame meant to a listener. Rather than being a time-consuming distraction from my all-important pre-med studying, the Glee Club rehearsals and concert tours actually cleared my brain periodically.

I remember with a chuckle one particular occasion when a Monday comparative anatomy exam coincided with a weekend-away concert. I was forced to bring my eviscerated cat on the bus in a plastic bag to study for it. My assigned hotel room became thick in every corner with the pungent odor of formaldehyde as I laid my tabby wide open before and after the concert. I wonder now whether that fetid scent was detectable on my white tie and tails. If so, it had to be nauseatingly admixed with 39 brands of aftershave and a smattering of BO. Perhaps that explains why Dean appeared to searchingly scan us on the risers for something untoward just before the curtain went up. My sickened Glee Club roommates were understandably less than amused and now good-naturedly lambaste me even today at our reunions.

During my three years in the Club, we travelled to many cities near and distant from the Golden Dome with me often cramming for my next pre-med exam to the roaring refrains of the Indiana Motor Bus Company engines. How worthwhile my catch-as-catch-can studying was, I'll never know, but I lived for those concerts singing and representing my University in front of countless alumni and subway-alumni and their families. Stage fright was not an issue for me having sung in front of an audience since age four. Dean made use of my rather strident voice, decent pitch, and "hamminess" by featuring me in some comedic songs and Gilbert and Sullivan's *Trial by Jury.* The rest of my Notre Dame years sped by with the Glee Club actually facilitating my pre-med studies. Returning refreshed from the concerts truly enabled me to concentrate with a clear mind and garner acceptable grades for admission to two medical schools and a place on the waiting list for a third.

Such a privilege to be in the Glee Club under Dean Pedtke could only make me love ND the more and look back on those days and that University with such affection. Though it would be reasonable to question the point, I felt myself every bit as much a Notre Dame man as any of our great athletes.

The University and the Catholic Church

Father John Cavanaugh,

Transubstantiation, and Notre Dame

John F. Fisher, MD (ND '65)

*Previously published in *Social Justice Review*, March/April 2005

He did not resemble Robert Prosky, the actor who counseled Sean Astin in *Rudy*. He was soft-spoken; small in stature. It was weeks into the senior theology course in which I was enrolled that I learned that our professor, John J. Cavanaugh, CSC, had been President of the University of Notre Dame. It was a classmate who informed me of the good father's erstwhile lofty status. Naturally, my admiration grew for this modest priest who might have regaled us with tales of Frank Leahy and Frank's many famous lads like Lujack, Hart, and Lattner and many of the renowned people he must have known in those glory years. Instead, Father Cavanaugh chose to focus us football-crazed nostalgics on the sacramental theology of the Catholic Church for at least three hours a week. Our text was the rather obtuse work of Edward Schillebeeckx, *Christ the Sacrament of the Encounter with God* which asserts that our seven sacraments are unique forms of interaction with the Supreme Being beyond that occasioned by private prayer.

According to Father Cavanaugh, the sacraments could take our relationship to the Creator of the universe to heights unimagined and each yielded its peculiar brand of a spiritual tonic called grace. Most of us in his course were self-assured, Notre Dame seniors, elder statesmen among the student body. Our Catholic high school religion classes were now but a shadow of a memory. To us, grace was some sort of intangible help from God. Further elaboration was impossible.

After regurgitating the *Baltimore Catechism's* definition of grace with a cotton mouth and in a cold sweat for Sister Mary "Inquisition" years ago, I had never given the subject much further thought and I doubt if any of my classmates did either. Most of us had gone to Mass every Sunday by rote since grade school (unless we were granted a reprieve by the ten-mile limit). We were oblivious of benefit from it. The outcome of Saturday's Southern Cal game mattered far more than receiving Communion the next day. Most of us still dragged ourselves out of our dorm bunks on Sunday and crept into the back of the church trying to pretend we had been there since the beginning. The ushers, who glanced at their watches and glared at us as we came in, knew better. Only the really militant snoozers or the hung over could sleep on Sunday mornings anyway with that clanging-err-joyful noise- coming from the belfry of Sacred Heart Basilica. My roommate and I were particularly filled with the spirit(s) on the Lord's Day on hearing the cacophony from that third-floor, turret-room in Sorin Hall on the side facing the church.

Looking back, one of the benefits of all those Masses and Communions as a youth *had to be* that we were to end up on that campus for four years of our lives. And I thank John Cavanaugh for helping us finally to realize, through the inscrutable Father Schillebeeckx, that in our sacraments we are spiritually participating in the life of God.

Through Baptism, we had become members of the Mystical Body of Christ with Him as the Vine and us the branches. There were no initiation fees or membership dues and we were certainly undeserving of this magnanimous gesture from God. What we never considered before Father Cavanaugh was that the cool water of Baptism actually confers the cleansing it signifies, liberating us from the consequences of Adam's sin by water more purifying than any Dasani® or Aquafina®. This washing, an act of Jesus Himself, enrolled each of our souls in a New Covenant with the Father and marked the beginning of our own journeys of sanctification.

All of us are aware of the dangerous curves and precipices along that road. Most have already found it strewn with boulders, rife with cacti and hundreds of land mines carefully concealed there by Satan alongside our good intentions. Consequently, for the rest our lives we need constant contact with Our Savior to protect us from harm. The remaining six sacraments provide that contact. They offer, not some vague spiritual confidence, but, if we are willing, they will tilt us permanently in the direction of God. Received with a contrite heart, the sacraments place in us a genuine longing for truth and goodness and because God is the source of all truth and goodness, a longing for Him of the sort Jesus had for his Father.

Given the power of the sacraments to transform our very nature, it is difficult to understand how a Catholic could not be interested in being so transformed. However, as much as God loves us, He will not force it on us. The graces of the sacraments may be strong tractor beams drawing us ever closer to the Almighty, but we can decide not to love Him back. His gift to us of our free will is ours to keep and to use against Him if that is our choice. Incrementally desensitized by what is portrayed in the media as normal or laughable, the moral relativism of society, and our own desire for pleasure, recognition, and things, we can opt out of the life Jesus lovingly offers through the sacraments and, of course, He would be free to opt out on us in the end.

Most of our Protestant brothers and sisters have been content with their own "personal relationship with their Savior," a kind of "you and I against the world, Lord" mindset. They have eschewed liturgical contact especially if it involves a priest. Romish rituals such as the Mass, it is claimed, are not scripted in the New Testament and are a false invention of man. Thus, there is virtually no sacramental life for most Protestants. Help from Jesus or God the Father for themselves or for their friends is sought in their own humble words.

Sacred Scripture is the only other source of crisis intervention available to the afflicted Protestant Christian and it is by far the most important. Their flawed notion of Catholicism is that we are directed by the Church's Magisterium and not by Scripture. They are not aware of our shared doctrine that reading of Scripture is a very real and grace-giving encounter with God. They would never guess that there is more Scripture at any Mass than at most of their Sunday services.

Most 21st Century Protestants have never considered the fact that the Bible was not available for mass consumption for decades after the invention of the printing press in 1445, nor that the faithful have been largely illiterate through most of the intervening centuries. Hence, only the upper and middle classes have had the Sacred Word for study and prayerful supplication and those only in the last 200 years or so. Indeed, much of the developing world is still unable to read making private reflection on favorite passages or chronological analysis unlikely. Therefore, a system of worship based upon *sola scriptura*--the belief that the entire body of revealed religious truth is contained in Scripture-- leaves a lot of people out in the cold. The irresistible irony is that there is at least one important omission in the Bible, namely a statement that it *is* the only source of that truth. Nevertheless, Bible study has not been available for most of the history of Christianity.

It remains unclear why biblical fundamentalists should really need further assistance anyway once they sincerely repent of their sins and give their lives over to Our Lord, Jesus; for that is when they know they are going to heaven. The significance of the event is such that many recall the precise moment they were "saved." And why would they not? What more could a Christian desire than eternal happiness without any punishment for past transgressions? Many do change their entire modus operandi from that point and begin an exemplary journey of progressive holiness. The majority, however, seem to remain like most of the rest of us Christians even after this epiphany, each day still chequered with the same old tendencies and battling the same old demons. Or is it demon?

Our inheritance from Adam tilts us so continually toward sin that it would be a momentous day indeed if we had not done something rather selfish or mean-spirited. For the saved Protestant minor or even major infractions--past, present, and future--are of little consequence. Emasculated, Satan might as well spend his time elsewhere. For the more vulnerable Catholic whose salvation is not a fait accompli, without continuing sources of God's grace, sin leads on to sin as way leads on to way and the devil remains quite a potent adversary.

Justified by a giant leap of faith alone, one could understand a Protestant's more than casual resemblance to the Pharisee who is confident about being among the elect and condemning the "rest of men" with his Catholic brother more like the contrite publican hoping for mercy. The former really needs no additional grace; the latter, a never-ending supply. Both of these positions cannot be true. One must be heresy.

Father Cavanaugh saw the sacraments as bounteous opportunities to narrow the vast chasm between man and God in concrete, not abstract, lines of communication. Each sacrament in its own way assured a relationship with Christ as close as possible to the physical one enjoyed by the apostles. The contact of the twelve with Jesus had to be one grace-giving event after another over the course of three years. Father Cavanaugh reminded the class that because Jesus knew we could not live in His time, He must have intended that we too could have real contact. After all, He ordered the twelve to make disciples of the rest of us (Mt 28:19). They did just that and made the sacraments a very visible part of that discipleship even before the death of the last of the apostles, John. Indeed, John did not write his gospel until after Baptism, the Eucharist, Holy Orders, and the Anointing of the Sick were in full vigor among early Christians. John could have proscribed any of these practices. Yet there is no hint in John's writings that he disapproved of the early Church's sacramentality. On the contrary, this is the evangelist who tells us that Jesus stung many of his followers with the suggestion that He *was* the Bread of

Life and that they should eat His flesh and drink His blood to live forever. Repulsed by such a concept, many left Him after that (Jn 6:67). John did not tell us that Jesus pleaded with them to come back or explain that He was only speaking symbolically. Father Cavanaugh jolted us with a new way of looking at daily Mass and Communion- that Jesus fully intended for us latter-day disciples to personally join His band of followers and have daily intimate contact with that Bread of Life.

Fourteen centuries later, when leather-bound Bibles became more plentiful and private interpretation of Scripture encouraged, the reformers were to forswear the sacraments and, tragically, even the Eucharist's pivotal role in daily worship. Surely they never really believed in the actual presence of Jesus in the consecrated bread and wine or they could never have forsaken Him and the Mass so cavalierly. In their view, Our Lord would have been pleased with their efforts to cleanse a 16th Century Church much in need of reform and "return" to a simpler worship style, never grasping that the baby had been thrown out with the bathwater. However, historically, they were returning to a format which never existed. Even if Protestantism was to be Jesus' preference, would He really have been content to wait 1500 years before we got it right?

The Reformation's focus on the individual and his Bible spawned today's 22,000-plus versions of Protestant Christianity although Jesus prayed that we would be one (Jn 17:11, 22). Presumably, He is still happy to hear from believers whether they call on Him from First Baptist, First Presbyterian, United Methodist, Assembly of God, or Church of Christ; but is this what He meant when He said, "And so I say to you, you are Peter, and upon this rock I will build My church, and the gates of hell shall not prevail against it. I will give you the keys to the kingdom of heaven. Whatever you bind on earth shall be bound in heaven; and whatever you loose on earth shall be loosed in heaven" (Mt 16:18-19)? With all binding and loosening since the Reformation, the difficulty some Protestants have had in finding a church is understandable.

Our lack of unity as the Body of Christ jeopardizes the relationship of the entire human race to Almighty God because Jesus had a particular plan for it. Unfortunately, since the Reformation the unbelieving world has seen only disparate doctrines or bitter and, at times, even bloody disputes among Christians and not a loving Jesus. Our house is so divided that many well-intentioned congregations actually send missionaries to developing Christian countries with the intention of converting the people to their brand. Is it any wonder that Christianity is not sufficiently appealing to non-Christians when we cannot agree on what is true?

In its eagerness to placate other Christian doctrines, Notre Dame has been an unwitting accomplice to the subversion of that truth. With his great love for the sacraments and his University, Father Cavanaugh would have been appalled. For what was begun there on an Indiana farmland in 1842 has become the premier *Catholic* university and the world is watching more than football. Good will and tolerance for opposing views is vital to any liberal education and should be vigilantly guarded by Notre Dame. However, with respect to our interaction with God and especially our reclamation, the nervous watchdogs of academic freedom should be called off. Luther's faith-alone-based instant ticket to paradise demands of God that He admit anyone "who says to Him, "Lord, Lord" bypassing those "who (do) the will of My Father" (Mt 7:21). A lifetime of doing His will is nigh impossible without His constant assistance. If Jesus is really present in the Eucharist and if He is God, this sacrament must be the greatest earthly source of that help and all people need access. Notre Dame cannot sit by in polite ecumenical acquiescence while our non-Catholic brothers and sisters miss out. Either our Church is infallibly guided by the Holy Spirit or it is not. The Eucharist is an indelible part of that truth. Though it could be argued that the sacraments are not a *sine qua non* for salvation, they certainly facilitate holiness if the Catholic understanding of justification is true, superfluous if it is not.

Incredibly, many Protestants believe that Catholics are not Christians. If one who holds this view or some other misconception about us is teaching physics or economics at Notre Dame, we can only hope that he or she will "know us by our love for one another." The matter is far more serious if that person is on theology faculty. Notre Dame's bright young people are likely to be much further advanced in math, science, history, and literature upon their arrival on campus than in religion. A Protestant scripture scholar whose church participates purely symbolically in the Lord's Supper once a month and is a dynamic, enthusiastic teacher, might well displace naive Catholic students far from the Magisterium of the Church and far from contact with Jesus in the Eucharist. To ignore this sacrament is to reject the Christ who is tangibly among us on our planet. If *sola scriptura* is the linchpin of Protestant theology, then the sacrament defined by transubstantiation is the linchpin of Catholicism.

The best universities hire theology faculty primarily on their publications. As a consequence, *sola scriptura* Protestants with those credentials may well be as plentiful as Catholics. In homage to the type of free exchange of ideas one finds at Harvard, Yale, or Dartmouth, such scholars have landed at Notre Dame. With respect to the arts and sciences, this approach has placed the University among the top academic institutions in the world. However, the truth about the Church which Jesus Christ intended to lead us to Him is at stake and its teachings are not just another point of view. Opposing doctrines should be presented in the spirit of academic excellence, but their flaws should be identified by Catholic apologists for impressionable young minds.

Four years at Notre Dame should point them to the Eucharist for the closest possible relationship with their Savior in this life. Notre Dame cannot brook heresy however appealingly or subtly presented. We are our young brothers' (and sisters') keepers when it comes to bringing them fully to "the Way, the Truth, and the Life." The University's responsibility also extends to our non-Catholic and non- Christian faculty as well. If all on that campus are not drawn to or at least curiously impressed by the remarkable sacramental Christianity taught and practiced there, something is terribly awry. Father John Cavanaugh, God rest him, most certainly did his part to help us appreciate the treasure which is ours in the Catholic faith. If we truly love others and desire that they too have the full measure of the life of God here on earth, we must make them aware of how important the Eucharist is to that life. Transubstantiation, intensively promulgated by Notre Dame for the reality that it is, may be the unexpected solution to the Christian unity the world has been seeking and perhaps even to "peace on earth, good will to men." The intimate mingling of ourselves with Jesus in Holy Communion is potentially that powerful!

With apologies to Grantland Rice[1], I pray that one day, "Outlined against a blue-gray October sky," the reality of the Eucharist will have "swept like the crest of a cyclone" over the Notre Dame campus and from that focal point on to the rest of the world. Otherwise, our university may become just another fine school which began as Catholic, but has become non-denominational.

NOTES

I. Grantland Rice. 'The Four Horsemen," *New York Herald Tribune,*
October 18,

1924

Gender Indifference at Our Lady's School— A View from the Grotto*

John F. Fisher, MD (ND '65)

*Published as "Notre Dame's Decline" in *Catholic Insight Magazine*, June 18, 2020

As she looks out over the troubled students, hundreds of candles, and the placid lake named for her, I believe Our Lady would tell us that hatred of others whose views and lifestyle differ from ours is always evil and inimical to living a holy life, if one is so inclined. When those views and lifestyle have to do with human sexuality, heterosexual people can be especially prone to condescension and censure of other choices. Yet there are challenges for all of us in this arena. Indeed, some of the current notions of gender happen to be in conflict with the anatomical reality assigned by their Creator. I will assume that those who chose to come to Our Lady's School believe in a Creator, but am open to the possibility that they do not. Nevertheless, various gender factions desire and even demand inclusion as normal members of the Notre Dame family along with the heterosexual majority. Hatred and bullying may well have been part of their experience with their own gender-identity struggles since childhood. Such mistreatment could conceivably have led them to find safety and comfort among persons of a similar persuasion. Without arguing for or against what is normal, how does personal holiness emerge from these seemingly vast differences of opinion? In short, how do we honor God with our gender?

Without a relationship with another human being, the human sexual drive creates an inner tension which seeks an occasion for release. Many would likely view as completely normal human behavior any sort of sublimation so long as neither or none of the participants are forced and no others' rights are infringed in the process. Virtually any variety of sexual activity would be acceptable to some groups in the spirit of "no harm, no foul" and they certainly would not obsess about same-sex marriage. However, any mention of Natural Law would likely be avoided because of the possible connection to any Legislator.

According to Catholic teaching which, I would assume, remains in full vigor at Notre Dame, it is impossible for God who *is* love (1 Jn 4:16) to do other than that which is loving and spiritually pure. In keeping with his nature, he equipped all of the earth's inhabitants with reproductive organs. To deny their obvious purpose is to deny natural law. It should be further emphasized on that co-ed campus that a man and a woman are made in the very image of God and have equal dignity. When infatuation between a heterosexual couple evolves into love, it is ideally assumed that each has recognized their affection for each other in the context of their personal and mutual relationship to God. When that happens, families and friends gather and ask him to make their union genuinely loving, grace-giving, and, especially, holy in the sacrament of matrimony. If God is involved, it cannot be otherwise. It follows that their sexual intimacy would also be an extension of his divine love. This transforms their sexuality into something which is not merely biologically ordered and pleasurable, but involves the couple's innermost dignity as human beings and children of God. Since all Christians are called to be open to God's will (Mt. 6:10), the physical union of married, Christian couples allows them to participate in his generosity, creative energy, and holy plans for them as husband and wife. Therefore, their union must be accepting of the possibility of God's greatest gift--the transmission of human life. Not unexpectedly, the Church views marriage as holy and permanent.

We Catholic heterosexuals can remove God and holiness from the equation with a casual, one-night "hookup," philandering either in person or on-line, getting involved in pornography, thwarting conception, and aborting our babies. For same-gender couples the word, love, has often been applied to a strong physical, emotional, or intellectual attraction. Such feelings are often genuine and not necessarily unholy. However, without God, their sexuality becomes little else than gratification from an orgasm following insertive or receptive anal intercourse or genital stimulation by artificial means or otherwise. Without a relationship to the Creator, there can be no Godly love in any of these aberrations.

All of us in the Notre Dame family are beckoned to true holiness because God loves us unconditionally, deserving or not. Although he doesn't force us, we are called to treat all of our brothers and sisters as Blessed Mother Teresa treated those dying in the streets of Calcutta. When asked why, she said profoundly and succinctly, "Because they are Jesus." Even those who would ignore or more forcibly take issue with Catholic moral principles at Notre Dame *are* Jesus in the same sense. However, their disparate views and way of life cannot be condoned or tolerated as an optional variant on a truly Catholic campus. They must be invited, without hatred, to take their disruptive propaganda under pain of expulsion to a secular university where they will be welcomed and even celebrated.

The University of Notre Dame, certainly not Our Lady, has failed us if we didn't take the religious component of our education to heart and didn't develop a desire to seek personal holiness from what some would argue is the number-one Catholic university on the planet. So what were we there for? If all we wanted is a successful and gender-indifferent life as society views it, we could have gotten that in an Ivy League whose universities only used to be founded on the teachings of Christ.

Best Golden Domer on Campus: A Fable in Search of a Reality

John F. Fisher, MD (ND '65)

Mary Kowalczyk was born and raised in South Bend. She came from a family of six children of whom she was second youngest. She had been a healthy girl growing up, but always slightly overweight for her age. She was rather plain and shy, but well-liked in her class by both the boys and the girls because she had an easy laugh and was a good sport. She didn't excel in either elementary school or high school and didn't have any aspirations for college. She married an automobile mechanic who left her a widow at 42 to raise their three children. They were now all grown and settled out-of-state and, at 55, she applied to the University of Notre Dame for a job in housekeeping since she lived near campus and had been a member of Sacred Heart Parish in the crypt of the Basilica on campus for 35 years and a daily communicant at the 6:45 AM Mass since her kids were gone.

Mary was as committed to her menial chores for Classroom Services as she was to her faith. Arguably, no one at Notre Dame took their work as seriously as she. She was determined to have her work area simply spotless for any student having a seat in one of the three, 400-seat classrooms to which she was assigned. And they were. Her motivation was first and foremost her love of Jesus and next, to provide a clean place of learning for all these bright young people for whatever profession they ended up choosing. Some of them noticed the pride that someone in housekeeping had shown in the shiny floors, but they didn't know her name since her shift was 11:00 PM to 6:00 AM. Only her supervisor knew that she was the very best he had ever seen in his 22 years.

"

Focuses on perfection like that of Mary Kowalczyk are commonplace on this campus of high-achiever types. Indeed, it has resulted in Notre Dame's number-one ranking of Catholic universities and institutions of religious studies. Moreover, Our Lady's school has become the 18th-best university in the U.S. and in the top 25 in the fields of philosophy (# 11), physics (# 22), law (# 24), biology (# 24), and history (#25). To be able to enter ND into one's curriculum vitae in almost any field is often a ticket to an elite graduate program, an enviable starting salary, and a comfortable life anywhere in the U.S. or abroad. Returning for Fall football games will almost always be a happy gathering of success stories for years to come.

But Mary's high energy is derived from a different motivation altogether. Hers is Jesus of Nazareth. Hers is the pursuit of a difficult- to-reach goal—holiness, and she strives for it in a simple, anonymous fashion. One wonders whether at this number-one Catholic university in the U.S. whether the top senior in the school of religious studies each year will have Mary's focus on Our Lord as the primary reason for learning. Is that person the brightest and most learned about religion with the most publications or the holiest? Is he or she a daily communicant with all that knowledge?

Will the editor of the ND Law Review defend or prosecute, evaluate contracts, present briefs, probate wills, and give business advice because of love for Jesus. How much work is *pro bono*? Will he or she call upon Thomas More for help in becoming the holiest lawyer in the U.S.?

Will the graduate ND architect who is number one in the class design buildings which are truly safe for occupancy and stay within budget mainly because that talent was given by God for the safety and well-being of the people who will live or work there?

How will the Emergency Medicine physician (ND 2012) treat the disheveled, belligerent drunk who comes to the Emergency Department at 3:30AM, confused and cursing, awakening him or her from sleep in the on-call room? Will he be viewed as "the least of these, my brothers" by this doctor?

All of us, most especially ND grads, are called to true holiness for the love of God; to treat our brothers and sisters as Blessed Mother Teresa treated those dying in the streets of Calcutta. When asked why, she said profoundly and succinctly, "Because they _are_ Jesus."

Such holiness cannot be achieved without an attitude like Mary Kowalczyk, who loved Our Lady's school, but did not get the privilege of higher learning from it. God's grace is what energized her, most likely in the basement of the Basilica every day. For the Eucharist is the linchpin of our Catholic faith. All of us proud Domers should have learned *at least that* on that storied campus. If we didn't take it to heart, then Notre Dame failed us. So what were we there for? If all we wanted is a successful life as society views it, we could have gotten that in an Ivy League whose universities used to be founded on the teachings of Christ.

Pushing Back Against the Current Culture

The Good Sisters: Restlessness in the Ranks

John F. Fisher, MD

*Originally published in *Social Justice Review*, March/April 2006

Where *is* a woman's place? The correct answer in 2004 is, "Anywhere she wants." Even to hint in favorable terms about the home may quicken the pulse and dilate the pupils of female activists, since any kind of subservient role for women simply does not compute today. And from a secular humanistic point of view, it shouldn't; for many of the women of the 21st Century are smarter, tougher, harder-working, and just better than their counterparts of opposite gender.

Women of ambition now make up large percentages of medical, dental, law, business, and engineering school class rosters and are ensconsed in the work force forever.

While most may be content with a challenging profession which pays a salary commensurate with training and ability and allows a reasonable private life, some women covet positions of leadership and recognition. Indeed, they are seeking public office in unprecedented numbers and getting elected. To suggest that it should be otherwise is to invite the wrath and venom of feminists, the scorn of women professionals, and the disagreement of most everybody else. Given the selflessness which would seem to be the heart and soul of a true vocation to the religious life, militant feminism among the good sisters, as they have been affectionately known by many, is mildly surprising. Some of these women are unexpectedly vitriolic and highly vocal as they eschew life in a convent, aspire to the priesthood, and demand equality for girls and women *now* in the Church, and with it, the right to offer Mass. Pope John Paul II with his orthodox leadership engenders wrath, rancor, and even open demonstration and defiance. He is considered by some to be an old man out of touch with the real issues of these troubled times, his authority and descendancy from Peter notwithstanding.

The watchword is power. It comes disguised in less inflammatory terms such as authority, recognition, influence, parity, strength, and equality; but it is power clear and simple and these women want their fare share. And rightly so on the most basic level, especially since many nuns are highly educated, talented, dynamic individuals. Many have keen insights, vast knowledge of scripture and theology, and organizational skills and leadership qualities far superior to some of the aging, burned-out men well past their prime who may celebrate Mass.

But is not power as much a "strange god before Me" as was Aaron's golden calf (Ex 32:8) whether it is sought by men or women? Males of our species have worshipped at the altar of this god for aeons, women only sporadically until now. Today, the scent of power is in the water and a feeding frenzy is about to ensue among the female sharks, sadly, even the good sisters.

But hold on a minute! What about this Jesus and His teachings over which we Christians, male and female, were once upon a time ready to be thrown to the lions? Where did He stand on issues of dominance, influence, strength, and authority? Jesus both started and ended His earthly life in lowly and humiliating fashion. Even His first appearance in His public ministry was submissive. John baptized *Him* of all people (Mt 3:16)! In language piercing with irony, this Jesus spoke of meekness and mercy (Mt 5:5,7), not clout and retaliation. He likened the Kingdom of Heaven to little children (Mt 19:14) suggesting that those who do not accept it like a child would not go to heaven at all (Luke 18: 17) and further indicating that the greatest in the Kingdom is a person with the humility of the little ones (Mt 18;4). This Man, whom we say we believe in, is the same person who washed the feet of His disciples and stated that it is the least among us who is great (Luke 9: 48) and if anyone would be first, that person should be last of all and servant of all. (Mark 9: 35).

Are we to conclude that these directives are outmoded, passe, and "no longer in touch with the real issues of these troubled times?" Can we reconcile our desires for high rank, high office, and recognition with these clear orders from the Messiah Himself? Perhaps men and women who actively and even hostilely demand opportunities for such station feel that Jesus was only *suggesting* that we put others before ourselves or that He was referring to someone else and not to us. It might be prudent to reconsider.

Well, someone has to lead doesn't he (or she)? Yes, and wouldn't it be refreshing if that leader surfaced without all the anger, hostility, and general flailing which goes on today; and, as a bonus, all in God's good time? Indeed, it is not at all improbable that through diligent study, a positive attitude, arduous labor, and real giving of oneself to others, a virtuous man or woman might be raised to a position of power and prestige, as part of the Grand Design. But haven't we lost our focus the instant these successes become goals in themselves? The moment we feel slighted, overlooked, unappreciated, and rejected when we have seemingly given our all for others is a moment in Our Lord's wonderful irony when we are supposed to celebrate, not demonstrate; for blessed are we (Luke 6: 20-38). If leadership and influence should come our way as a result of our earnest efforts to see our mild and gentle Savior in everyone, our humility must then shift into high gear because it is His doing, His grace, more than our own ego-massaging accomplishment which has put us there. Ironically again, only when we recognize our own unworthiness to be in charge, can we hope to set the example which will lead others to spiritual greatness.

Our noble interests and talents are gifts to us from above and, as such, it cannot be wrong to nurture and develop them (Mt 25: 14- 30). Accordingly, should a person have the inclination and ability to become a physician, a lawyer, a stockbroker, a professional athlete, a priest, or a nun it is not necessarily wrong to pursue it. But is it not also true that our chosen profession should be the forum in which we can best serve God and others? If God is not even part of the equation by which we choose our life's work, shouldn't He be? Presumably, for men and women opting for the religious life, God is the numerator, the denominator, and the solution the equation--or was once upon a time.

Someone who can create the universe should have no problem understanding the ambitions, the strengths, and the failings of each of His creatures. Does God not know about every breath we draw? Therefore, it is illogical to think that each of us would not have a significant role in His orderly and eternal drama. How the drama will unfold may depend not on how angry and vocal we have been in demanding larger and larger parts, but, ironically again, on how well we have heard and believed His Son as loving members of the supporting cast. It was not His intention that women consecrate bread and wine. In the meantime, we men and women--dare we suggest even the good sisters? --have enough on us trying to accomplish our assigned duties, trying to see the Jesus who looks out at us from the eyes of everyone in our path today, trying to turn our grievances, envy, and frustrations into love today; decreasing ourselves while He increases in us today. Tomorrow is His concern.

How to Destroy the Family in Six Easy Lessons--The Beelzebul Method

John F. Fisher, MD

*Originally published in *Catholic Insight Magazine*, October 19, 2017

I am known by many names like Beelzebul, Mephistopheles, or Satan. When I was created, God called me Lucifer, but I prefer-- Prince of Darkness. He literally fired me before the Big Bang for my arrogance, selfishness, and disobedience and banished me forever to Earth after it came into existence. For this reason, I detest God and always will. When the first humans arrived, God implanted in their laughably primitive intellects a desire to seek him, somehow without forcing them. Vindictively, I designed a perfect plan to thwart their efforts to regard him as a loving father. I have never before revealed my skullduggery, but it is working almost perfectly except for a few misguided souls. I'm looking for allies—people who are mad at the world, want to take what life here has to offer, and give nothing back. Let me tempt you to join me in my vendetta by showing you what I've done so far.

Since the strongest instincts of human beings are self- preservation and propagation of the species, I have targeted the family for destruction. Although my strategy will continue to take some time to complete in earth years, it was well under way by their 20th Century using these six easy steps:

1.   Send the men off to war.

Playing upon the natural tendency of humans to covet the land and property of others, over the millennia, I have successfully influenced the strong leaders of tribes to try to conquer other lands and people. Some hostile tribes welcomed the challenge; others were simply trying to protect their families and country in "just" wars. Before the 20th Century, my task was more difficult because most of the world was still uncivilized and a family often consisted of men with several wives and many children. By 1900, in powerful countries the industrial revolution produced the nuclear family with a working husband, a stay-at-home wife, and three or four children. So, I planted hatred based upon selfish interests and paranoia among the leaders of some of these countries and, in 1914 and again in 1939, aggressors and defenders sent thousands of young men to war never to return. Happily, wives and children were often left to fend for themselves and mothers entered the work force just according to plan. Grandparents who often lived with their children by this period in their lives tired easily, but were left to do much of the child rearing. They already tended to spoil the kids and to be less strict, so I didn't have to interfere. Unexpectedly to some, but not to me, the mothers were as good or better at the jobs vacated by the men. When wars ended, husbands returned to new jobs as the economy flourished, and many women remained successfully employed. Families soon became accustomed to two incomes—needed or not. Infants and children continued to be cared for by relatives. The destruction of the nuclear family had subtly begun.

Contrary to my design, many post-war children were born and families remained large and tight-knit. These poor saps often congregated around the radio listening to nauseating programming like the The Lone Ranger, The Shadow, Gunsmoke, and Dragnet where evil never triumphs over goodness like I made certain it often did in the real world. With respect to movies, thanks to the sanctimonious watchdogs of the National Legion of Decency, on- screen love affairs were sickeningly saccharine and had none of the gratuitous violence I advocated. When it came along, television was even more repulsive with productions like The Jack Benny Program, Father Knows Best, The Adventures of Ozzie and Harriet, The Andy Griffith Show, and The Jackie Gleason Show. My bathroom and bedroom humor were taboo. Writers were forced to create clever dialogue, situations, and characters which at times, even made me stifle a laugh. A happy result I hadn't expected was that the shows were often so well done, families became less interactive, sometimes passively staring ahead as if watching a fire. Furthermore, televisions were still luxury items often requiring two incomes and keeping Mom out making money instead of nurturing her young ones. Yes!

2. Foster population control.

Preposterously, pregnancy out of wedlock was still considered a disgrace in the 1930s, 40s, and 50s and many couples decided to marry if that happened. The common folks had more children and most stayed together. Because abortion-on-demand was not yet legal, rich and famous pregnant women went off somewhere, had their babies, and, according to plan, put them up for adoption. Sex remained pleasurable, but having babies was inconvenient for competitive, successful women.

Before 1930, Christian churches uniformly forbade any form of artificial contraception. Thanks to the influence of my unwitting racist, Margaret Sanger, championing the cause for birth control, the Anglican Church's Lambeth Conference opened the floodgates in that year with their approval "provided that this is done in the light of the Christian principles" (LOL) and now virtually all mainstream religions allow and even encourage it, except for that confounded Catholic Church.

Fostering totally unfounded fears about worldwide starvation, I helped hoodwink John D. Rockefeller and his sons and grandsons into aggressively promoting population control by underwriting "scientific" research and publications on overpopulation and funding major universities, even some Catholic ones. The *quid pro quo* to receive the generosity of the Rockefeller Foundation required course content promoting fear of overpopulation of the planet and subtly shedding a more favorable light on contraception in their curricula. However, my *piece de resistance* was urging Katherine McCormick to supply the money, and Gregory Pincus and John Rock to develop "the pill," and approved by the FDA in 1960.

Responding superbly to my temptations in that same decade to produce films which glamorize sex for obscene profit such as *The Apartment*, *La Dolce Vita*, *Lolita*, and the hugely popular Ian Fleming adaptations, *Dr. No*, *Goldfinger*, and *From Russia with Love*, the common folks became increasingly desensitized to extramarital trysts. After all, their "role models" on the big screen weren't concerned. Why should they be? The pill virtually eliminated any fear of an unwanted, "shotgun" pregnancy and dealt another blow even to an imperfect concept of family. *Humanae Vitae*—Bah! Humbug!

Men have always been rather pitifully predictable creatures with simple, one-track minds—even as patriarchs of a family. In the traditional families of the 19th and early 20th Centuries, most men had few focuses: pay the bills, take care of household chores requiring manual labor and simple repairs, fill that empty feeling in the stomach with something, keep mother happy to at least limit whining and complaining, spend an hour or two with the kids, dull the senses with strong drink, release sexual tension, and spend the remainder of the time idling or on a hobby of some kind. My many strategies to vary the emphasis on one or more of these over the years has quite successfully promoted family disharmony. Women, however, anything but predictable, complex creatures, are instinctively driven to keep the family intact. Their husbands' sexual appetites didn't change, but the availability of the pill allowed a married couple to conveniently choose the number and timing of any offspring. The entire focus of sexual intimacy shifted after 1960 to pleasure. Comforted by the endorsement of virtually all non-Catholic religious groups, there was little "danger" of conception, thwarting any creative plans of the Enemy. I also managed to keep fairly secret from many devout believers the fact that the pill might work in part by a "mini- abortion." As a happy spinoff of widely available oral contraceptives, my temptations toward married people to philander also began to work better. Take that, one big happy family!

3. Promote gender equality

Working women were not amused by caricatures like being kept barefoot, pregnant, and chained to a stove and the "modern women" of the mid-20th Century were becoming increasingly discontent. Betty Friedan's *The Feminine Mystique* clearly articulated a rage held by some, and women's lib became a workforce cause. The torch of anger and frustration at inequality among the sexes was carried forward by Gloria Steinem and my favorite anarchist, the braless Germaine Greer. My skillful, negative influence on their parents had given these very bright, attractive women an unhappy and dysfunctional childhood making them angry at the world and at traditional families. They scoffed at publications like *Ladies Home Journal* and the sexually segregated, help-wanted advertisements. Their impact on impressionable young women first surfaced in that misguided civil rights movement of the early 1960s and in community politics where trade-union women were beginning to lobby for equal pay. Both Gloria and Germaine have expressed that bitterness in so many delightful ways through the years that I have great plans to thank them someday unless Someone finally gets through to them.

Anger against traditional women's roles in society turned to rage on college campuses like Smith College and the University of California at Berkeley— two of my favorite bastions of "progressive thought" and some of their charismatic, radical professors converted many to the ideas of the great Karl Marx. Senator McCarthy had incurred the wrath of many of their heroes of the big screen in the 1950s so that most of Hollywood, if not already Communist, had moved to the far left. To their fans now in their late teens they could do no wrong on-screen or off. The draft lottery for the Viet Nam war brought young men with low draft numbers into the women's cause. Anarchy became more and more popular and there was no shortage of crowd agitators for burning draft cards and bras.

4. Pollute the Popular Culture

According to Almeria in William Congreve's play, *The Mourning Bride*, music traditionally was supposed to have "soothe(d) the savage breast," but with my influence and their raging hormones, Bill Haley and the Comets' *Rock Around the Clock* and Elvis Presley's *Hound Dog* and *Blue Suede Shoes* ignited young people. The strident sounds of 'rock and roll' may have begun among white, rock-a-billy bands, but black youths, instinctively musical and rhythmic, soon became a tour de force in the genre with frenetic Little Richard and groups like The Orioles and The Diamonds. Parents who had danced to Glenn Miller and Count Basie were bewildered by the cacophony of "The Bop," "The Chicken," and "The Stroll" which turned their kids into juvenile animals. About the same time, young, upstart professor Timothy Leary was proclaiming the gospel of "tuning in, turning on, and dropping out" which coincided quite nicely with the developing anarchy of young people. New rock groups emerged with countercultural names like Led Zeppelin, Kiss (???Knights in Satan's [my] Service), The Grateful Dead, and Jefferson Airplane.

With the draft looming and pop icons making hit songs like Edwin Starr's, "War," and "I-Feel-Like-I'm-Fixin'-to-Die Rag" by Country Joe and the Fish, I helped head shop owner and music festival promoter, Michael Lang, and a group of his fellow hippies to follow through on their idea to organize "An Aquarian Exposition: 3 Days of Peace & Music," better known as Woodstock. Fueled by the festival documentary shown in theaters everywhere, hard rock, bohemian attire, and long hair became the standard for high-school yearbook photographs and created a world revolution in clothing and drug experimentation. Communes, love-ins, and my basic philosophy about humans, "If it feels good, do it" and "free love" became quite hip. Few of the young people could really articulate what they were for or against, but quite according to plan, the sexual revolution was in full swing. Shabby military-surplus clothes became the style, but the body odor and hairy legs of hard-core feminists didn't last long among the 20-somethings and their adolescent protégés. Soon they would be in clean fatigues, braless like anarchists, but with radiant, long hair, subtle makeup, deodorant, and fragrances like *Shalimar*®. A majority of the girls dressed up for this masquerade whose parents could afford it, were "regularizing their menstrual cycles" with the pill. The danger of conception was down, but the STD clinic business was happily booming.

However, there was one pregnancy that I applauded, the third (and thanks to me, unwanted one) of Norma McCorvey who, as Jane Roe, went all the way to the U.S. Supreme Court to petition for a legal abortion in 1969. Unfortunately, she delivered her baby before the 1973 decision and, even worse, she later eschewed the part she played in it along with her lesbian lifestyle, and joined the dratted Catholic Church. Despite her prominent role in the Pro-Life movement, the abortion horse was let out of the barn and today we are up to more than 700,000 exciting dilatations and curettages a year. As you might imagine, I'll do whatever it takes to keep that horse from ever returning. Long live the culture of death!

5. Promote Careers over Motherhood

The wars of the 20th and 21st Centuries have proven that women are as capable as men in almost every profession. The answer to the question, "Where is a woman's place?" in the current millennium is, "Anywhere she wants." Even favorable reflections about home life and children are apt to quicken the pulse and dilate the pupils of my women activists who have cemented the notion among many modern women that motherhood is second-class citizenry. I have fostered the idea by enticing driven, female college and graduate students into becoming highly successful in careers in law and science. It is now commonplace to find women as editors of law reviews, district attorneys, professors of medicine, and department "chairs" at prestigious institutions. (I successfully influenced the PC police to expunge the term, "chairman," years ago.) Some of them have lengthy bibliographies and relish the often phony stature which accompanies it. Many have become quite attached to the accolades and fawning by their admiring women students and trainees. I have convinced them that they are more intelligent than most women and that their influence in the world, not the home, is of paramount importance. Many would never deign to be a mother since it is beneath a woman of their intellect. Unfortunately, I have not been able to stamp out the idea of having children from most young women—professional and otherwise-- and some single mothers have to work. But for those who insist on having children, I have heavily promoted an alternative strategy—day care. Children who spend most of their formative hours with baby sitters, short on education and making minimum wage, fit perfectly into my plan to produce dysfunctional children since they are devoid of genuine nurturing by an intelligent mother who loves them more than her work outside the home.

6. Promote Families without Fathers

Ingeniously, since the latter part of the 20th Century, I have been able to successfully distort the natural ability of humans to make joyful sounds and rhythms which the Enemy gave them instinctively. My truly inspiring sexual revolution and that ridiculous civil rights movement helped greatly. Formerly anathema among serious songwriters, lyrics soon began to contain uninhibited, implicit or explicit sex acts in heavy metal, disco, 'Motown', jazz, and country music. With the advance of computers and sound technology with affordable drum machines, rhythm-centric music like rap (aka hip- hop) with its deceptively creative and simple, spoken iambic pentameter emerged. Singing at all or even on key was not required, but an angry, ebonic voice was. Thanks to the racial paranoia I had fostered after the Rodney King beating by some very bad (good) cops and with special recognition to the Bloods and Crips, Ice-T, and Schoolly D, 'gangsta rap' emerged as a mainstream form of hip-hop. Bass tracks from car CD players blared at 100 decibels and passively aggressively vibrated all cars within a city block. The rappers unashamedly rhymed about violence, guns, murder, drugs, and rough hypersex. The contagious beats were decried as loud noise to a large segment of the population, but were sweet music to my ears! Most were not terribly affected, but, happily, some young black youths look up to these "cool dudes" and begin to act and dress like their music- video mentors. My same magic worked with the head-banging, moshing, heavy metal for the mostly white, gothic crowd. I couldn't have been more pleased with teenage girlfriends of all colors having baby after baby and bringing them home to mama with the fathers nowhere to be found. If my plan isn't thwarted by Someone, the next generation should be even more dysfunctional. My chances of this happening in the entire population is enhanced by celebrities and high-profile sports figures of all ethnicities who have multiple, live- in lovers for a few months or years with offspring from each affair. The question, "Who's your daddy?" couldn't be more real. What's more, unmarried musicians, movie stars, and athletes with children are celebrated not only by my media minions like the producers of E!, but lately also by mainstream television. My special thanks to Brad and 'Angel'ina, and Goldie for the example they set. Who needs married, male role models who are good providers and love and guide their children with the help of their wives in the direction of the Enemy?

Banishment by God has kept my anger and resentment at fever pitch since humans first came here and will never end as I'm sure you have gathered from these six ongoing and highly successful strategies of mine. His great affection for these pitiable creatures is beyond me. But if I can keep successfully deflecting the juggernaut of his confounded grace, they are definitely mine and the family cannot survive. However, if these numbskulls ever realize that their Creator is actually here on earth now, I am done. Many of them give lip service to desiring a personal encounter with God for themselves and their children. I must not let them discover that since around 33AD, that encounter is now possible daily in the Eucharist of the Catholic Church if they want it. At that infernal Supper of the Lamb (ie Mass) he changes the substance of wheat bread and wine into himself. It is his most powerful weapon against me because when they receive, he becomes part of them for a time and, like a tractor beam, affectionately draws them to himself and to holiness. I am determined to hide the real meaning of the Lord's Supper from other believers or simply vilify it through my "virtues" of anger, jealousy, and resentment for the Church left over from the 16th Century. In the interim, I have so obfuscated the truth through individual interpretation of the Bible that there are now thousands of versions of the Reformation, but none with the tangible Jesus. With the destruction of the family, no one will really care and by the next few generations bibles should begin to gather dust and church attendance, especially by Catholics, should continue to fall off dramatically.

If, after reading this, you like my work, come join me in the fight. You may not realize it, but you may already be helping me in one or more of these six prongs of my pitchfork.

Your devious friend,

Beelzebul

Against Organized Religion? How's The Weather Outside It?

John F Fisher, MD

Previously published in *Catholic Insight Magazine*, January 19, 2018

In 1999, it was estimated that 24 million Americans—almost one in 10—do not admit allegiance to any particular faith denomination according to a four-year study of the religious orientation of adult residents of the United States conducted by Scripps Howard News Service and Ohio University. According to the Pew Research Center, between 2007 and 2015, the percentage of persons not affiliated with any religious denomination rose from 16- 23 %. Of these unaffiliated, the percentage who believe in God fell from 70-61%.

If you are one of the many who have eschewed organized religion, it was most likely for one of several reasons—it was not part of your upbringing; church services are boring; your own inertia; you are a secular humanist and have no genuine conviction about the existence of a supreme being anyway. Alternatively, you believe in God, but have complete confidence in your own simple, honest, and direct path to the creator through an uncomplicated and, in your view, pristine set of beliefs.

Additional ammunition you use for opting out of "church in a building" is because of the hypocrisy and arrogance you have encountered among priests, bishops, ministers, rabbis, mullahs, and their seemingly brainwashed flocks. Furthermore, the horror of September 11, 2001 shrieks of yet another perpetration of man's inhumanity to man in the name of religion and most organized religions seem to have been guilty at one time or another be they

Catholic, Protestant, Jewish, Muslim, Sikh, or Hindu. What's more, pedophile priests, womanizing evangelists, and bearded men in strange headgear who view women as inferiors and won't eat pork turn you completely off. If that's what church, synagogue, or mosque is today, you reason, you want no part of it.

You particularly pride yourself on your non-judgmental, inclusive, live-and-let-live outlook. After all, you are a decent sort of person, pray reasonably often, and involve yourself in a variety of personal and civic charitable activities when asked. That's enough isn't it?

Maybe not, if you are willing to take a hard look in the mirror. If your reflection shows you someone in an easy chair with a beer in one hand and TV remote in the other, selfish with his time, tight with a dollar, irritable in traffic, short-fused on the golf course, impatient in lines, or disgusted with panhandlers and everyone on welfare and you've been this way as long as you can remember, you will have to admit that, at least, you are not making much progress. There is some comfort in the fact that most of your friends are a lot like you. But it would be quite a stretch to blame your torpor as a human being on lack of membership in a particular faith tradition.

Even if belonging to some worshipping group could get your life moving again, how can you choose among thousands? If you are even willing to shop around, you must eventually come to some conclusion about this man, Jesus, just to narrow the field. There is no question that he is an historical figure even in the unlikely event that the New Testament is pure fantasy. He lived on this planet. His sentence for his teaching was a most ignominious type of capital punishment, crucifixion. Those are facts which exist outside of "sacred scripture." Here it is of interest that the writings which Christians refer to as gospels depicting the life of Jesus were written in Hebrew about six years after Jesus' crucifixion (Matthew), in either Latin or Greek about four years later (Mark), in Greek, 24 and 63 years after the death of Jesus (Luke and John, respectively). With the impressive ability that time has to erase memories, the congruities these four separate biographies possess are no less than astounding. Even if you are a professor of American history at Harvard University, what can you spontaneously recall, for example, about the lives of Abraham Lincoln or Robert E. Lee?

Similarly amazing is the impact that this one individual had on the human race after only three years of public life without the means of modern travel, cell phones, the internet, newspapers, radio, and television. Yet the world's calendar somehow came to be based on the life of Jesus. What's more, one in three of us six billion people on this planet profess to be his followers. His message of love of God, love of neighbor, and forgiveness rather than retribution seem hardly enough to have produced such fame. Surely, there must be more to it.

C.S. Lewis, a famous Anglican Protestant and erstwhile atheist, in his *Mere Christianity*, reasoned with remarkable clarity that either Jesus was crazy, a terrible liar, or he was who he said he was. Ultimately, he came to the conclusion that Jesus is the Messiah the Jewish people had been waiting for—and the Son of Almighty God.

If after reading Lewis or others, you become convinced that Jesus and not Muhammed or Buddha is the answer or if you had already considered yourself a Christian, which form of Christian worship most reflects what Jesus intended for his followers? There are still more than 30,000 from which to choose. Maybe it's even the form you now practice on your own minus a weekly haranguing sermon. But before arriving at that convenient conclusion, wouldn't it be worthwhile to investigate how the apostles and their followers in early Christianity worshipped?

If you think this a reasonable approach, like it or not, you now must confront that paradigm of organized religions, the oldest Christian sect on the planet, the Catholic Church. What with its altars, statues, crucifixes, incense, rosaries, priests, brothers, nuns, bishops, cardinals, popes, confessionals, standing, sitting, and genuflecting, it is canon fodder for the unbeliever. On the other hand, this is the church of some famous Christians—Patrick, who converted the pagan Irish; Augustine, former reprobate and author of *Confessions*; Joan of Arc, heroine of the 100 Years War; Thomas More, chancellor under Henry VIII; Francis of Assisi, friend of wildlife; and Thomas Aquinas. Aquinas is acknowledged even by opponents to have been one of the most brilliant theologians and greatest minds the world has ever known. Were these singular Catholics simply misguided and mistaken in their understanding of their founder's master plan? Two of those mentioned and many others were martyred for their faith. How unfortunate to die for a Church whose doctrine is false!

Reformation Protestants actually witnessed or heard first- hand of real abuses which had crept into the church to which they belonged, but at least they understood the liturgy and were going to Mass on a regular basis. Luther and Knox were Catholic priests! These and other reformers knew full well that their church had been the standard bearer of Christianity for the previous 1500 years. Most had no major doctrinal issues with the Church. In many cases, it is unfortunate that their constructive and valid criticisms fell upon deaf papal ears and resulted in excommunication from the Church. The understandable reaction to such a sentence would be bitter vitriol against Rome. Thus abruptly disenfranchised, many reformers vindictively determined to separate themselves from any semblance of priests and papism. Could it be that in their blind rage, they threw the baby out with the bathwater attempting to reform and purify the Church?

In any event, as a consequence of the Reformation and the diluting effect of 500 years and the now thousands of Protestant denominations, modern-day Protestant Christians know next to nothing about the Mass in which their forefathers had once been active participants and today dismiss it out-of-hand as preposterous, meaningless ceremony. These are genuinely good Christian people who are taught to be skeptical about anything they can't specifically document in sacred scripture (*sola scriptura*, ie scripture as the only source of Christian truth). Indeed, intensive study of the bible as an encounter with God's word and therefore with God himself is more than encouraged; it is expected. A typical day in the life of a Protestant Christian begins with individual reading of some passages from scripture, reflection, and prayer seeking to attain a more "personal relationship with their savior." A typical week includes a much anticipated, stirring sermon from the pulpit and some resounding, old-fashioned hymns on Sundays and Wednesday nights, and a bible-study fellowship involving just a few or hundreds depending on the church. These activities provide the fuel for the zealous to involve themselves in wholesome individual or family projects, charitable activities, and evangelization to "spread the good news" around the globe. In the view of most Protestants, this is Christianity distilled to its essence. Complicated, repetitious ceremonies involving the offering of bread and wine to God the Father like the Mass seem foreign to these good people and certainly not needed for worship. If this was ever part of their heritage, some reason, it is well that it disappeared from most Protestant services in the 16th Century. Good riddance! All that is needed is God's word. However, most would squirm slightly as they consider the irony that nowhere in the entire bible is it stated that scripture is the only source of truth about God. Indeed, St. Paul says quite the opposite: "So then, brethren, stand firm and hold to the traditions which you were taught by us, either by word of mouth or by letter" (2 Thess. 2:15). Thus, according to the bible itself, the notion of *sola scriptura* should be heresy.

But don't Protestant Christians have a point about all the altars and candles, priestly vestments, and general pomp and circumstance surrounding the Mass? Isn't all that a little much? Not according to Scott Hahn, a former Presbyterian pastor in his book, *The Lamb's Supper*. In this work, Hahn reminds the reader that Jewish worship involved the offering of sacrifice to God as an acknowledgment of his sovereignty over all. This usually involved the burning of domestic animals or sacrificial wine on an altar. However, two sacrifices in Genesis deserve reflection--first, the willingness of Abraham to sacrifice his only son, Isaac (Genesis 22). This is seen by many scripture scholars to foreshadow the offering of Jesus by his Heavenly Father (John 3:16). Of note next is the first priest mentioned in the bible, a man named Melchizedek (Genesis 14) who was also a king. This odd combination of priest and king would later be applied to Jesus. Genesis describes Melchizedek as king of Salem, a land that would later become (Jeru-) Salem meaning city of peace. Jesus would arise one day as high priest and king of the heavenly Jerusalem and again like Melchizedek, "Prince of Peace." Melchizedek's sacrifice was extraordinary in that it involved no animals. He offered bread and wine, as Jesus would at the Last Supper when he took bread, gave it to his disciples and stated quite categorically, "Take and eat; this is my body"... Then he took the cup filled with wine and stated again, "Drink from it all of you; for this is my blood of the covenant which will be shed on behalf of many for the forgiveness of sins."(Mt 26:26- 28) "Do this in memory of me." (Lk 22: 19) Strangely and quite unpredictably, a literal interpretation of these particular words is abhorrent to even the most scripturally fundamentalist Protestant denominations.

However, the Catholic Church holds and teaches that the ceremony conducted by Jesus at the final Passover of his life was not merely symbolic. A transubstantiation or change of substance had occurred. The unleavened bread and wine had become his actual body and blood (the "Bread of Life"—Jn 6:35) which he gave to them to eat. Jesus then is considered by Catholics to have been the celebrant at the first Mass and ordered his disciples and their disciples' disciples to repeat this ceremony. Thus, on the four corners of the globe virtually all Catholic priests have been pronouncing the words of Jesus over the bread and wine every day at Mass for nigh onto 20 centuries fully convinced that the bread and wine are no longer mere bread and wine, but Jesus himself under the form of bread and wine. An analogy of this change of substance would be that of an American flag, originally just fabric, but once the stars and stripes have been added, never again simply fabric, but always our national ensign. The worthy reception of this seder meal, according to Catholic doctrine is then a sacramental encounter with the Messiah of 2000 years ago. For those who could not live in his time, Jesus considerately left them a way of being able to tangibly experience him in a grace-giving event. His disciples received his grace to live holy lives directly in their daily personal contact with him. Catholics who understand their faith believe that, like the twelve, they too can experience that "personal encounter" with Jesus today and every day of the year at Mass if they so desire.

Was this function of "priests of the order of Melchizedek" (Hebrews 7:17) unwittingly "thrown out with the bathwater" by Renaissance Protestants in their all-too-human rage against a Church which truly needed some cleansing and a return to basics, but whose all-too-proud hierarchy wouldn't listen?

You may view consuming a morsel of unleavened bread and sipping wine like this in a ceremony such as the Mass as ludicrous and certainly unnecessary for worship. And you would be right-- unless Jesus is the Son of God and literally meant what he said. Could these very ordinary works of human hands become the true gift of himself to those of us who were to come later in time? If so, how could any Christian snub such a gift? How could a true follower of Jesus stay away? The earliest Christians certainly took it very seriously [1 Corinthians 11: 29]. By and large, Protestant traditions have chosen not to. One wonders whether this choice has its roots in hurt, anger, hatred, and vindictiveness left over from the 16th Century rather than a genuine desire to purify and simplify the worship of God. If Protestants were at all willing to take a critical look at church history, they might be chagrined to find that the early Christian church did not look very "Protestant". Thus, if by some quirk, transubstantiation is a reality, those Christians who choose not to participate at Mass and go it on their own are certainly not evil, but they might be missing out on daily opportunities to have the most personal of "personal relationships with their savior." If Catholic liturgy is analyzed as revolving around this belief in the Real Presence of Jesus himself on the altar at each Mass, the pomp and circumstance, the glorious music of Bach, Brahms, Beethoven, and Mozart, the priestly vestments which reflect Jewish high priests of old, the incense at high Masses, the bowing and genuflecting before the Creator Of The Universe are quite appropriate. Moreover, its basis in scripture is rock solid and very old harkening back to an ancient Jewish heritage--a heritage that Protestants have all but abandoned. If the passages of scripture from his last supper are to be taken quite literally, as Catholics believe, the Mass and the celebration of the Eucharist, as it is called, have to be man's highest form of worshiping God, period.

On the other hand, if you are certain that Jesus didn't mean precisely what he said, or you regard the concept of the Real Presence as absurd, why be a Catholic? And if you are already a nominal Catholic and don't believe or understand the doctrine of transubstantiation, get out!—for the Eucharist is the linchpin of the Catholic faith and a Protestant tradition will more than suit your needs if you want to belong to a Christian church. One only has to look at Christians like Albert Schweitzer, Florence Nightingale, Billy Sunday, William Jennings Bryan, Helen Keller, C.S. Lewis, Billy Graham, Martin Luther King, Jerry Falwell, and many others to realize that the Catholic Church certainly does not corner the market on genuine followers of Jesus.

And now, back to you who have not chosen to belong to any formal believing body. If your unorganized approach to religion is not making you more joyful, more grateful, longer-fused, more generous with your time and money, and giving your life more meaning, it may be time to "regroup". If it is not generally narrowing the gap between you and Almighty God as the years go by, maybe you, too, are missing out of some grace-giving events available in the congregation nearest you. The words of the Lord's Prayer indicate quite clearly that worship is not solely to be an individual endeavor. It is not "you and I against the world, Lord." The words are not "*My* Father who art in heaven...Give *me* my daily bread and forgive *me my* trespasses". The rest of us belong in there with you as the community of believers. Many of us are part of an organized religion and worship together in a building or even a tent somewhere. So maybe, just maybe, you ought to come inside and get out of the rain.

Misunderstanding, Catholicism--

A Primer for Catholics and Other Christians or "I'm

OK, You're OK"
John F. Fisher, MD

*Originally published in *Catholic Insight Magazine*, August 13, 2019

I pray not only for them, but also for those who believe in me through their word, so that they may all be one, as you, Father, are in me and I in you, that they also may be in us, that the world may believe that you sent me. (Jn 17:20-21)

It is long past time for federal and state governments to remove the words, 'Catholic' and 'Protestant' from all forms. Wouldn't Christian, Jewish, Muslim, Hindu, Sikh, Buddhist, and 'Other' be better? All of us are focused on the divine, but the word, 'Protestant' suggests a different target: The Catholic Church.

And as for my non-Catholic, Christian brothers and sisters, why should some government form define you as opposed to Catholicism by labelling you, 'Protestant?' I'm open to the possibility that a few of you are quite anti-Catholic and want the label, although I'm not certain why. Perhaps this quote from Bishop Fulton J. Sheen is fitting for those who are still protesting and even angry, "There are not one hundred people in the United States who hate The Catholic Church, but there are millions who hate what they wrongly perceive the Catholic Church to be." But most of you have Catholic acquaintances, dear friends, or even relatives and I genuinely doubt that you hold their brand of Christianity against them or even give it much thought.

Most Christians of other faith traditions have perhaps been to a Catholic wedding, but have never been to a Mass and have no desire to go. And that's okay too. Those who have been present for our liturgy most likely recognized many of the readings from the Old Testament, the letters of Sts. Paul, Peter, James, and John, and the Book of Revelations at the beginning of the service. They feel comfortable standing and listening to the familiar gospel passages. They join us enthusiastically in the Lord's Prayer—that is until we abruptly stop after "deliver us from evil." Catholics in the crowd can almost sense the blushing as their doxology, "For thine is the kingdom…," trails off into an embarrassed silence. However, with the exception of "Take this and eat of it" and "Take this and drink from it" they are bumfuzzled by most of the rest. This is especially true of all the kneeling, standing, sitting, genuflecting, and the seemingly obsessive "cleaning up of the dishes" after communion. Moreover, they don't understand why they are not invited to the Lord's Supper and perhaps even annoyed by the snub.

Annoyance is perhaps understandable, but most devout Catholics are bewildered by the outrage of a few who have fashioned a lucrative career out of attacking "Romanism" from the pulpit or in print. They rail at our "graven images" and "worship" of Mary and the saints, scoff at confessionals, and ridicule us for working our way to heaven. Most of our Christian brothers and sisters are not openly critical and vitriolic like these few, but have accepted without question that this is the way we worship.

Lest they think we have gone off the deep end in our prayer life and beliefs, an explanation first of what Mass (aka Eucharistic celebration) is all about may be enlightening. The word Mass comes from the Latin word *missa* which means dismissal referring to the end of our liturgy. It refers to the 'mission' or 'sending' of the participants at the conclusion of the worship service. The last words spoken by the priest when the celebration was in Latin were "Ite missa est"—"Go forth, it is the dismissal." Nowadays in all the languages of the world, the priest says something like "Go forth in peace to love and serve the Lord"—a pretty ecumenical sendoff.

The structural elements of the Mass were described in the second Century by Justin Martyr in an extensive letter called *First Apology* (to "The Emperor Titus AElius Adrianus Antoninus Pius Augustus Caesar, and to his son Verissimus the Philosopher, and to Lucius the Philosopher, the natural son of Caesar, and the adopted son of Pius, a lover of learning, and to the sacred Senate, with the whole People of the Romans,") in about 155 AD. He explained what Christians did on Sunday. First, they all gathered together and listened to the writings of the prophets and apostles. The priest (L. *presbyter*) challenged those present to imitate the principles they heard. The people then rose and offered prayers for themselves and all others everywhere. Hopefully, nothing untoward so far. This was followed by bringing bread and a cup of water and wine mixed together to the priest who offered praise to the Father through the Son and Holy Spirit in thanksgiving (Gr. *Eucharista*). Those present then consumed the "eucharisted" gifts and took them to those who were absent—a hint that these gifts were not ordinary bread and wine.

The modern Catholic liturgy of the word and Eucharist are considered one single act of worship of the Father taking place at the table of the Lord—the altar. The Mass is a renewal (a non-bloody, re- presentation) of Jesus' sacrifice of Himself. There was only one bloody sacrifice to God the Father as the Passover Lamb for the sins of the entire world, past, present, and. future --ie once for all (Heb 10:10). During the seder meal the night before, Jesus said to his apostles "Take this and eat. This is my body and take this and drink from it, this is the cup of my blood. Do this in remembrance of me" (Lk 22:19; 1 Cor 11:24-25). Catholics take those scriptures quite literally (Jn 6:32-59) and have faithfully followed this command celebrating the memorial of his sacrifice.

Today's Catholic priests are ordained to "the Order of Melchizedek" (Gen 14:18-20; Ps110:4; Hebrews 7;1-28), a priest and king of Salem (peace), who offered to God a unique sacrifice of bread and wine. This is one of the many examples of Jesus, king of (*Jeru*-- new) Salem being prefigured in the Old Testament and revealed in the New. Using the words of Our Savior and his directive, in the Mass the celebrant priest asks the Holy Spirit to change what used to be ordinary bread and wine into the very Body and Blood of Jesus—a transubstantiation. Moments later, the priest raises these consecrated elements—now Jesus himself--up toward God the Father with these words of worship, "Through him (ie Jesus), with him, and in him in the unity of the Holy Spirit, all glory and honor is yours, Almighty Father, for ever and ever." And the congregation says what is considered the great "Amen." Assuming for a moment that this change of substance actually occurs, there would be no more perfect offering than the Son himself in an un-bloody sacrifice to God the Father in worship. With our belief that Jesus is present on the altar, it is not at all surprising that the Catholic focus is there for most of the liturgy.

That the bread and wine were special parts of the offering was articulated as early as 56 AD by Paul (1Cor 11: 23-7) when he wrote, "…Therefore whoever eats the bread or drinks the cup of the Lord unworthily will have to answer for the body and blood of the Lord." Evidence that the early church fathers carried on this Sacred Tradition can be found in the writings of Ignatius of Antioch. In his letter to the Smyrnians in 106 AD, he wrote: "…They even abstain from the Eucharist and the public prayer, because they will not admit that the Eucharist is the self-same body of our Savior Jesus Christ, which [flesh] suffered for our sins…" Ignatius was a disciple of Polycarp, who learned from the apostle John himself. In *First Apology* Justin Martyr had more to say about the sacredness of the offering, "…the food which is blessed by the prayer of his word, and from which our blood and flesh by transmutation are nourished, is the flesh and blood of that Jesus who was made flesh."

That same 'Word' made flesh in what was formerly ordinary bread and wine has been offered in adoration to God the Father and then received by the congregation in the Supper of the Lamb

(Revelation 19:6-21) at every Mass all over the world since then. In many non-Catholic services the bread and wine (or grape juice) are reverently and prayerfully received in the Lord's Supper, but the recipients regard it as a memorial only. Irrespective of whether non- Catholics believe whether Jesus is tangibly present or simply symbolically, it is still a grace-giving event for all of us, Catholic and non-, who receive with a contrite heart.

If the bread and wine (or grape juice) are only symbols, one cannot desecrate them as they are being handled and anyone is invited to receive. However, for 2000 years the Church has consistently taught that in the elements consecrated by Jesus's words, he is truly present – body, blood, soul, and divinity. And what if the Catholic interpretation is correct? Good Christian people from other faith traditions who are present, but who do not believe that, cannot then join us in our unified belief in a truly Holy Communion. Our reception is an outward statement of our unity of faith--that we are united (communing together) to one another in believing in all that the Catholic Church believes, teaches, and confesses. It says with the body, "I am a Catholic; that I therefore unite myself to Jesus and his Catholic Church, through the bonds made in the Eucharist." It is the very linchpin of our faith. Those who are not Catholic cannot make such a declaration, because they are not fully in communion with us. So, for a non-Catholic to receive Communion, however reverently, would say outwardly, "we are one", when we are not.

It is not a judgment about anyone's salvation, nor is it about how sincere someone may believe in Christ. The Church also limits communion to just Catholics out of concern for the spiritual well- being of non-Catholics after Paul's admonition in scripture that to eat the bread or drink the cup of the Lord without discerning the body and blood, is to receive condemnation. (1 Cor 11:27). This would put that person in spiritual danger. Sadly, far too many baptized Catholics are also in spiritual danger when they approach the Supper of the Lamb casually without genuine understanding and reverence.

Our belief in the Real Presence, then, explains the handling of the consecrated elements and their receptacles with supreme reverence and fastidious cleansing because they contain, in our view, God the Son. Unconsumed, consecrated bread is then housed in a tabernacle for later worship services. Indeed, there is a devotion, not widely known to non-Catholic Christians, called Perpetual Adoration. Available in some Catholic churches, in this unique form of worship outside of the liturgy, a wafer of consecrated, unleavened bread from a recent Mass is housed in a monstrance (a gold receptacle with a clear glass center). The monstrance is then placed in a side chapel in plain sight where Christians of any denomination are invited to pray, read, or simply be present in contemplation with the Good Lord himself at any hour of the day or night throughout the year. The scriptural precedent for such a devotion is from Jesus's agony in the garden— "Could you not watch one hour with me (Mk 14:37)?

Regardless of whether Perpetual Adoration is offered, Jesus is tangibly present in most Catholic churches at all times. Genuflecting before the King as we enter the pews for Mass or simply to pray in a visit to the church is scripturally the right thing to do (Philippians 2:9- 10). There are still a few of us who make the Sign of the Cross when we pass a Catholic church because of our belief that he is there. And if he is there, how could you stay away?

Now about those "graven images" and worshipping Mary and the saints. Many Catholic churches contain statues and stained-glass images from the old and new testaments depicting holy persons. The omnipresent image in a Catholic church is a crucifix (the corpus— body of Jesus--nailed to a cross) behind the altar. Non-Catholic churches have a simple cross to remind them. Nevertheless, the crucifix in Catholic churches does not come close to depicting the suffering and humiliation Jesus went through on our account. In the real event, Jesus was likely nailed to the cross clothed only in a loin cloth because nudity in 1st century Jewish culture would have brought shame to the Jews watching him struggle. The Romans perfected this form of capital punishment and designed it to maximize pain and produce horrific suffering and asphyxiation. Our crucifixes give us a more graphic glimpse of the sacrifice of the Lamb. Such a 'graven' image helps remind us what he went through for us.

The unfathomable love of our Creator for us sinners and his mercy has undoubtedly placed many or even most of our ancestors and deceased relatives and friends with him in Heaven. We call them saints even though we know that they were far from perfect. Catholics and non-, recite our belief in the *communion of saints* in the Apostles Creed. Catholics have a special day in the Church calendar, November 1st—All Saints Day, asking any or all of them to pray for us like we may well have done when they were with us down here. Are they not still living members of the Mystical Body of Christ or did they lose their membership once they died? Can they not pray for us?

Few of our non-Catholic brothers and sisters give the concept of the communion of saints much thought. Nevertheless, it has been part of Christian doctrine since the Fourth Century. In an encyclical entitled, *Lumen Gentium*, Pope Paul VI reaffirmed and explained the meaning when he said, "Being more closely united to Christ, those who dwell in heaven fix the whole Church more firmly in holiness. .
. . For after they have been received into their heavenly home and are present to the Lord, through Him and with Him and in Him they do not cease to intercede with the Father for us, showing forth the merits which they won on earth through the one Mediator between God and man…Thus by their brotherly interest, our weakness is greatly strengthened."

In contrast to most of our deceased relatives and friends, there are many Christians throughout the history of the Church whose holiness was sufficiently legendary and authenticated that they have been formally canonized as saints by the popes over the millennia. A declaration by the pope that a deceased person is unequivocally a saint is never taken lightly. Since the 16th Century, prior to an official proclamation, a detailed investigation of the life of a person proposed for sainthood takes place. The Catholic Church actually has an official who is part of the investigation for that very reason. It is an office that is often referred to as "Devil's Advocate," but is given the official name of *Promoter Fidei* (L. promoter of the Faith). There are many official activities that go on out of public view in the canonization process. The cause for canonization includes the content of their writings, overwhelming evidence of personal holiness, miraculous occurrences attributed solely to them after death, and many other considerations.

All documents of the canonization process must be scrutinized by this official and his assistants. The problematic issues and doubts he raises over the supposed virtues and miraculous events related to the life and relics of the candidate are laid out before all who are involved. It is his duty to suggest natural explanations for alleged miracles. He may go so far as to suggest human and selfish motives for deeds that have been accounted as heroic virtues. The cause for canonization is ended if these cannot be satisfactorily answered.

The Church calendar is replete with "feast days" of such canonized persons. On these designated dates, the celebrant priest offers the Mass and asks for the prayers of the saint for God's help to all the congregation. For example, June 22nd is the feast day of St. Thomas More, an English lawyer and Chancellor of England during the reign of Henry VIII. The final years of his life were depicted in a Broadway play by Robert Bolt and later an academy-award-winning movie, *A Man for All Seasons*. More was beheaded by Henry for treason in opposing his self-appointed title as Head of the Church in England in the aftermath of his divorce from Catherine of Aragon and marriage to Anne Boleyn. As a martyr for his belief in the sanctity of the marriage bond and the authority of the pope as a successor of St. Peter, More was canonized in 1935 by Pope Pius XI and is considered the patron saint of lawyers. A Catholic lawyer today might ask any one of us to pray for him or her and hopefully we would be happy to comply. But what about Thomas More? Did he, too, lose his membership in the Mystical Body of Christ when he died? As a special friend of

Our Lord, can he not pray for a troubled lawyer here on earth who might ask him for help? Or is this lawyer restricted to asking for the prayers of living fellow lawyers? Are we not all commanded to pray for one another (James 5:16, 1 Timothy 2:1)?

Many Catholic Churches are named for these special friends and often have a statue or icon of the saint to remind us of their devotion to Christ and seek to imitate them. For example, there are innumerable St. Mary's Churches around the world replete with statues and images of Madonna and child. Would any sensible Christian doubt the special love Our Lord had for his mother or question whether she is with him in eternity? Even discounting the many miraculous happenings related to her over the centuries, can we not ask for her special communication with her Son in our behalf as we do when we say, "…Holy Mary, Mother of God, pray for us sinners, now and at the hour of our death?" Surely, a rational person cannot call this worshipping her. Nevertheless, from a Christian perspective, she is arguably the greatest woman who ever lived.

Despite the commission to forgive sins or retain them (Jn 20;19-23) and prominence of confession in the early Church, most non-Catholic denominations do not accept this practice, arguing that all sins by the contrite Christian are forgiven only by God and a priest cannot discern the heart of the penitent. The Church's interpretation of that passage is that Jesus delegated the authority to his apostles and those they ordained. While it is true that only God can forgive sins and he does so as soon as we ask, some sins are deadly (1 Jn 5:16-17) and require of a Catholic a formal confession in the hearing of a priest. The priest acts by the power and authority of Christ to forgive sins conferred to him through his ordination. Jesus, Himself, discerns the heart of the sinner in the confessional. To have the humility and courage to confess sins openly to another is an occasion of grace for the penitent and another grace-giving encounter with Jesus. Thus, an additional opportunity for grace is the real reason for the Sacrament of Reconciliation. Are not all of us saved by grace (Ephesians 2:8-9)? It is not only scriptural, but a partial help to lead a holy life. John Paul

II confessed weekly, though the Church requires it only yearly. Whether it is truly beneficial is worthy of discussion among interested Christians, but for most Catholics the humility required is genuine. We believe this sacrament gives us God's help to avoid repeating these sins when we are truly penitent.

Finally, we are instructed by St. Paul to work out our salvation with fear and trembling (Philippians 2:12). We certainly do not "work our way to heaven" with this admonition and the Catholic Church has never taught this. Our faith and good works are wrought by God's grace. Sinful as we are, all Christians are in constant need of it. The apostles' physical contact with Jesus, their God and Savior, had to be one grace-giving event after another over the course of three years. Jesus knew that we, his 21st Century followers, could not live in his time. He must have intended that we, too, could have genuine contact with Him. He ordered his apostles to make disciples of us (Mt 28:19). They did just that and made the sacraments a very visible part of that discipleship even before the death of John, the last of the apostles. John did not even write his gospel until after Baptism, the Eucharist, Confession, Holy Orders, and the Anointing of the Sick were in full vigor among early Christians. John could have proscribed these practices, but he did not.

The Catholic Church teaches that the sacraments are grace- giving sources of a special and personal encounter with the Jesus of two millennia ago. They are designed to narrow the vast chasm between man and God in concrete, rather than abstract, lines of communication. Each sacrament in its own special way assured a relationship with Christ as close as possible to the physical one enjoyed by the apostles. Like the contrite publican (Luke 18:9-14), sinful Christians need a never-ending supply of his grace. Catholics get that help by reading scripture, going to Mass, receiving him in Holy Communion, formally confessing our sins, and responding to the graces which they bring by loving others.

None of our varied interpretations of scripture and Sacred Tradition pose a real threat to the salvation of our souls. Unfortunately, the Christian unity, which Our Blessed Lord prayed for (Jn 17:20-23), is jeopardized by arguing among ourselves and by far too many examples of mutual misunderstanding. No wonder so many non-Christians are not buying what we are trying to sell! The real argument for unity is the finished work of Jesus on the cross and his resurrection. Christians of all stripes most certainly believe that. His command that we love one another is available to all of us through the many sources of grace. Not to do so is to deny why he died, no matter how you celebrate the Passover feast. We have been a "house divided" for far too long. It's high time for all Christians to soften the pride we cling to in our own denominations, come together, and reach out to the non-believers whom Jesus loves like he loves us. Hopefully, Our Blessed Lord will forgive us until we can become one and judge us with his mercy. An 18th Century prayer like that of St. Alphonsus Liguori (with modifications) seems an appropriate close for a plea for unity:

"We love you, our beloved Jesus; we love you more than ourselves; we repent with our whole hearts for having offended you. Never permit us to separate ourselves from you or each other again. Grant that we may love you always; and then do with us what you will." (From *The Way of the Cross*)

Unnatural Family Planning
John F Fisher, MD

*Originally published in *Catholic Insight Magazine*, November 20, 2019

In a conclave of atheists, agnostics, and secular progressives, a seminar to discuss the human sexual drive would certainly speak about the most anatomically obvious purpose-- continuation of our species. Instinctive mutual attraction and mating between gender opposites (with or without a formal ceremony) seems directed to that purpose. Defying easy definition, the word, love, might be applied to the strongest physical, emotional, or intellectual attraction, but another synonym, if they could find one, would be preferred. Without a relationship with another human being, the human sexual drive creates an inner tension which seeks some sort of release. Our discussants would likely accept as completely normal human behavior any sort of sublimation as long as neither or none of the participants are coerced and no others' rights are infringed in the process. Virtually all nuances of sexual activity would be acceptable to the group in the spirit of "no harm, no foul" and they certainly would not obsess about same-sex marriage. A discussion of Natural Law would be avoided because of the possible connection to any Legislator. Continuation of *Homo sapiens* aside and regardless of how sexual tension might be released, any measures which prevent unwanted pregnancy as long as they are not physically harmful to the potential parents would likely be sanctioned by this group. As their intellectual inferiors, we who believe in God would be best served to opt out of such discussion groups since we since we cannot convince the intelligentsia about our primitive views.

Sadly, if we were to hold a seminar to discuss the purpose of sexual intimacy, we are far from united in our own beliefs. Indeed, we are probably less so than atheists. For some of us are firmly convinced that sexual intercourse is permitted only to a couple of opposite gender who are legally married by exchanging vows to each other and to God until separated by death. Others would be in agreement if the reference to death could be eliminated. Still others, some of them bishops, would be inclusive of couples of the same gender who are in a monogamous, loving relationship. Polygamy would be cited as biblical by a few congregations, but bestiality would be viewed by almost all as deviancy. A sizable group would consider masturbation completely normal human behavior and not at all sinful, while others have confessed it to a priest many times.

These varied opinions among us believers beg a burning question, "Is our God understanding and tolerant of our diverse approaches to the sexual drive He gave us or does He expect us to rise above the pursuit of orgasmic pleasure and use our sexuality as part of a loving relationship with Him?"

If we can explain why He, who needs nothing, made us in the first place, perhaps we can begin to answer that question. In reviewing the doctrines of some of planet earth's different religions to explain our existence, there is a common thread. According to the Catholic Church's 1885 catechism, "God made me (us) to know him, to love him, and to serve him in this world, and to be happy with him forever in heaven." The 1994 revision is more detailed: "The desire for God is written in the human heart, because man is created by God and for God; and God never ceases to draw man to himself. Only in God will he find the truth and happiness he never stops searching for: 'The dignity of man rests above all on the fact that he is called to communion with God. This invitation to converse with God is addressed to man as soon as he comes into being. For if man exists, it is because God has created him through love, and through love continues to hold him in existence. He cannot live fully according to truth unless he freely acknowledges that love and entrusts himself to his Creator.' "

Reformation catechisms employ the following language: "God created us male and female in his own image to know him, love him, live with him, and glorify him" and further, "We are created to be loving companions of others so that something of God's goodness may be reflected in our lives".

Muslims explain man's existence this way: "And I did not create the jiin (genies or spirits) and humans except they should worship me." [Quran 51: 56]. Thus, according to Islam, the essential purpose for which humankind was created is the worship of God.

Jews would summarize their teaching on the subject as follows: "The purpose of human existence is to achieve closeness to God. This is attained via living in accordance with the 613 commandments because each mitzvah (commandment), in its own unique way, contains the means for man to forge a relationship with God"

Thus, some sort of subordinate relationship with the Creator is the unifying theme behind the major religions of the world as to why we are here. We are created for God. Furthermore, he must have intended that each of us exist, not as some toys to amuse him, but because we creatures are the focus of his all-loving nature. Not apparently wanting to force that love on us, his most complex living forms on this planet, he allows us to tilt in his direction or away from it; for separated from even the highest animals is the vastly greater degree of freedom of choice possessed by *Homo sapiens*. We can choose to seek him and return that love or not. For those of us who are interested in a relationship with the Creator, we are likely to desire that for our children, who are presumably just as intended and precious to him as we. If the Good Lord intends that they be born too, sexual intercourse becomes far more than the mutual affection and pleasure experienced by a married couple. Moreover, the release of sexual tension by any means available conflicts rather perilously with God's grand design.

The Creator's purpose can be found in the first chapter of Jeremiah: "Before I formed you in the womb I knew you, before you were born I dedicated you.…" and in Psalm 139: "…you knit me in my mother's womb." Given these messages from the Almighty, and that fact that what is released in semen contains 20 to 150 million spermatozoa per milliliter, the marriage act becomes a component of an intimate and truly holy encounter with the Creator and His greatest gift—human life. From the perspective of the Catholic Church, artificial means taken to interfere with that gift is like saying to God, "No thanks; return to Sender." "We are interested only in our pleasure as a couple this time. We, not You, will make the decisions about any Jeremiahs, Beethovens, or Einsteins coming into existence."

Once prohibiting any form of contraception, the truth has apparently changed for Protestant Christian denominations. The vast majority are largely now acquiescent, tolerant, or even encouraging of the practice. A summary of some official stances follows.

Anglican and Episcopal Church

Despite denouncing the practice in 1908, the Church of England was the first to sanction artificial contraception at the 1930 Lambeth Conference with these words, "'Where there is a clearly felt, moral obligation to limit or avoid parenthood, complete abstinence is the primary and obvious method, but if there was morally sound reasoning for avoiding abstinence that the Conference agrees that other methods may be used, provided that this is done in the light of Christian principles."

(Questions: Are early withdrawal, the use of a condom, oral contraceptives, "morning after pills", or the placement of intra-uterine devices done in the 'light of Christian principles? And what exactly are the 'morally sound' reasons for avoiding abstinence?)

Baptists

The Southern Baptist Convention holds and teaches that the use of birth control, as a means of regulating the number or to space out the ages of children is a moral decision that is left up to each couple provided that the method used does nothing more than prevent conception.

(Question: Is the Baptist couple certain that God would agree with their moral decision?)

United Methodist Church:

Methodists, the second largest Protestant denomination, hold that every couple, not only has the right, but has the responsibility to control conception according to the circumstances in which they find themselves. Their 'Resolution on Responsible Parenthood' requires that the community and parents make all possible efforts to ensure that every child is born, not only healthy, but into an environment in which a person's full potential may be realized. Accordingly, Methodists support public funding for family planning services.

(Question: How do the parents know what is the environment leading to the achievement of full potential and is this full potential in the world or as a disciple of God?)

The Presbyterian Church

The largest denomination of Presbyterians (Presbyterian Church USA) fully promotes access to contraceptive options for all married couples. Indeed, the church has been an advocate for laws requiring insurance companies to cover the costs of birth control. The denomination holds that contraceptive services are part of basic health care and have an unfavorable view of unintended pregnancies because of the higher rates of infant mortality and maternal morbidity, and threats to the economic viability of families. The second largest denomination (Presbyterian Church in America) is pro-life, but has no official position on contraception. Nevertheless, many Presbyterians have been urging Congress and the president to include comprehensive family planning in any proposal for national health care.

(Question: Is an 'unintended pregnancy' any less a child of God and would the 'contraceptive services' the Church would allow include hormones which may function in part by preventing implantation of a fertilized ovum? And for the Presbyterian Church in America: Is 'no official position' a lukewarm acceptance?)

The Lutheran Church

In 1954, The Evangelical Lutheran Church in America stated that "to enable them to more thankfully receive God's blessing and reward, a married couple should plan and govern their sexual relations so that any child born to their union will be desired both for itself and in relation to the time of its birth."

(Question: How would a homosexual clergyman or woman pastor of the ELCA advise a same-gender couple regarding the planning and governance of their sexual relations to 'enable them to more thankfully receive God's blessing and reward'?)

Non-Christian religious groups now also support artificial contraception although the language of advocacy may differ.

Judaism

Jewish Law has traditionally opposed birth control or abortion when practiced for purely selfish reasons. The first mitzvah found in the Torah is to "be fertile and increase"--that a home without children is a home without blessing. However, Judaism also believes that as long as a couple is planning to have children, the spacing of births by contraception does not violate Jewish law. However, some methods to prevent conception are not permitted because of the injunction against "the destruction of seed." (Gn 38:8-9). Thus, the use of condoms is prohibited, while Orthodox rabbis have no objection to the use of the "pill". Nevertheless, Judaism, especially in light of the Holocaust, has generally encouraged having many children. The minimum number of children one must have to fulfill the mitzvah "to be fertile and increase" is disputed among rabbi scholars. Some say that one must have at least two children; some at least one of each gender.

With respect to the more liberal Reform Judaism: Again, birth control or abortion is opposed if done for selfish motives, but not if pregnancy is a health hazard to the mother or child, or when previous children have been defective or born into extreme poverty, where living conditions are inadequate or a threat to the welfare of existing children in the family. Indeed the Central Conference of American Rabbis (Reform) has declared that birth control is a necessity under such conditions. Liberal Judaism has no problem with condom use.

(Question: Did the Jews exsponge God's command to increase and multiply and subdue the earth [Gn 1:28; Gn 9: 7] and demur on His promise to "make your descendants as numerous as the stars in the sky [Gn 22: 17]?

Islam

The Qur'an contains no directives regarding contraception, although Muslim scholars have declared the practice permissible under certain conditions: 1) both husband and wife consent; 2) permanent sterility does not result unless it is done as a medical necessity; 3) the body is not harmed; 4) the quality, health, and sustenance of the family is aided.

(Question: Who decides questions about the quality and health of family life?)

Hinduism

Hindus believe in karma, the law of cause and effect. Karma results in thoughts, words, and actions which determine the destiny of the immortal soul. After death, all souls will evolve through many cycles of rebirth until all karmas have been resolved and moksha, a state of relative perfection and freedom from reincarnation, is attained. In recent years, the Hindu concept of *dharma, the right way of living,* has expanded to include the idea that personal choices affect the common good. Large families may be important, but producing more children than a couple or the environment can support is not for the "good of the world" but a harmful form of greed that violates *ahimsa (to do no injury) which defiles the harmony of the universe.*

(Question: Is the harmony of the universe defiled if a Hindu couple have an unintended pregnancy?)

Buddhism

Fertility is favored over birth control in traditional Buddhist teaching because Nirvana is only possible for a soul after it has existed in a human being. Birth control necessarily places a limit on the number of human souls hoping to reach Nirvana. However, if a couple believe that having additional children would be too burdensome on them or on the environment, they would find support for appropriate family planning in a Buddist teaching known as *The Middle Way* which reasons that good governments should provide contraceptive services for those who want them.

(Question: Would a devout Buddhist approve of the contraceptive services of Planned Parenthood?)

Chinese Religions (Taoism, Confucianism)

Evidence of family planning and use of contraceptives goes back thousands of years in China. Chinese religions emphasize the importance of directing an individual's life to peace and harmony — the ultimate goal of all human life. Perfection in these qualities leads to immortality in some interpretations of these philosophies. Family planning was never the choice of the couple; rather, one's social obligation was to have more or fewer children as demanded by the common good. Too many or too few children can upset the peace and harmony in society. The People's Republic of China endorses many components of these ancient beliefs and in the present age, population control has become an integral part of government dictates. The official family planning policy restricts urban couples to only one child. Rural couples may have a second child if their first was a girl. Although gender-directed abortion and infanticide are illegal, both still occur and, according to one report, by 2020 men will outnumber women by 30 million perhaps resulting in societal unrest and emigration.

(Question: Does death of the unborn or newly born females seem like a recipe for a peaceful, harmonious China for the future?)

Roman Catholic Church

According to Catholic doctrine, it is impossible for God who is love (1 Jn 4:16) to do other than that which is loving and spiritually pure. In keeping with his nature, he equipped all of the earth's inhabitants with reproductive organs. To deny their obvious purpose is to deny natural law. It is further taught in the Catholic Church that a man and a woman are made in the very image of God and have equal dignity, each in a different way. Ideally, the courtship should be far enough advanced that each has recognized their love in the context of their personal and mutual relationship to God. When that happens, they gather their families and friends together and ask him to make their union truly loving, grace-giving, and holy in the sacrament of matrimony. If God is involved it cannot be otherwise. As his special creatures, it follows that their sexual intimacy would also be an extension of his divine love. Because of Catholic marriage commitment, sexuality is transformed into something which is not merely biologically ordered and pleasurable, but involves the couple's innermost dignity as human persons and children of God. Since all Christians are called to be open to God's will (Mt. 6:10), the physical union of married Christian couples allows them to participate in his generosity, creative energy, and holy plans for them as husband and wife. Therefore, their union must be accepting of the possibility of God's greatest gift--the transmission of human life. No wonder the Church views marriage as holy and permanent!

However, the sanctity of sex is nullified by artificial contraception because its intrinsic, procreative nature and openness to God's will are deliberately thwarted. Such defiance, however gently rationalized, is considered immoral because the conjugal act was designed by God to be symbolic of a total, mutual self-giving of one partner to the other. It cannot be total when they contracept, because the couple holds back the gift of their fertility.

In his 1968 encyclical, *Humanae Vitae,* Pope Paul VI expressed concerns about the fallout of widespread artificial contraception. It seems his fears are eerily coming to pass.

There would be an increase in conjugal infidelity and a general lowering of standards of morality. The young especially would be tempted.

Quoting various sources, Tara Parker-Hope wrote that the data reveal that approximately 10 percent of married people admit to having had sex outside their marriage yearly and that in the course of their marriage 30% of men over 60 and 15% of women have been unfaithful. Perhaps playing a role in rising infidelity, especially in younger couples, is the ubiquitous access to pornography on the Internet which has been shown to affect sexual attitudes and perceptions of "normal" behavior. Moreover, there have been dramatic changes in how men and women relate to each other. More couples are living as if they were married and having children if they are so predisposed, but without the certificate and without the censure of society. Indeed, babies born to sports and entertainment celebrities are today most often celebrated in the mass media. For those who do marry, 40-50% now divorce.

Young people are not only being tempted, but approximately 80-90% of college-age students now engage in sexual activity of a diverse nature. Furthermore, a "hookup culture" has become part of campus life for 70-80% of the students. Hookups are generally defined as having three main features: a) various sexual acts; b) couples not in committed relationships; c) short-term interactions not signifying that a permanent commitment will begin.

Man would lose respect for woman and treat her as a mere object of pleasure.

The sexual objectification of women has become rampant in the U.S. and the developed world. Society is now inundated with depictions of women in commercials, prime-time television programs, movies, music lyrics and videos, magazines, advertising, sports media, video games, and internet sites. Women are now commonly shown in sexualizing and objectified manners, wearing revealing and provocative clothing and portrayed in ways that emphasize their body parts and sexual readiness or serving as decorative objects. The media often depicts a narrow and often unattainable standard of women's physical beauty and links this standard with a woman's worth. Moreover, research indicates that one in four women have been victims of rape or attempted rape, and more than half of college women have experienced some type of sexual victimization. It is small wonder that this has led to dangerously adverse psychological outcomes such as depression, post-traumatic stress disorder, increased body shame, appearance anxiety, and eating disorders for women of all social stripes.

It would be a dangerous

weapon in the hands of public authorities with no heed for a moral life.

In an effort to control the population, China had a one-child policy for more than 30 years. Parents without siblings are now permitted to have two children in a relaxed policy, but as mentioned above, practices of forced abortions, involuntary sterilization, and infanticide still occur. Lest the reader think such policies would be unconscionable in the U.S, the state of North Carolina sterilized more than 7000 people between 1929 and 1974 for a variety of reasons such as laziness, promiscuity, epilepsy, mental illness, or mental retardation.

A belief would emerge in man that he had absolute dominance over human life and to genetic engineering.

The science and legal practice of *in vitro* fertilization has led many infertile couples to believe they may become parents of an ideal male or female child of their choice. Many are unaware that, in the process, fertilized ova with undesirable attributes including gender are discarded. Moreover, genetic testing via amniocentesis can target human embryos and fetuses with developmental abnormalities or even of the wrong gender for termination of the pregnancy.

Thus, the pope's concerns were not unfounded given the "unnatural family planning" which has followed his encyclical on the sanctity of human life.

The rhythm method of contraception was introduced in the 1930s following the clarification of the ovulatory cycle by Knaus and Ogino in the previous decade. These gynecologists simultaneously discovered that ovulation occurs approximately 14 days before the normal menstrual period. In his book, "The Rhythm of Sterility and Fertility in Women" a Catholic physician, Dr. Leo Latz, described the method, but it may be unreliable for women with irregular periods. Evolving from this concept, natural family planning or fertility awareness programs have been developed for couples to recognize when they are most likely to conceive a child which are surprisingly as accurate and as effective as oral contraceptives, but without adverse physical or moral side effects. Accordingly, self-control is required on the part of married couples to avoid sexual intercourse during the relatively few days when ovulation is occurring. For a couple whose marital relationship to God is undeveloped, abstinence may be challenging. It is certainly possible for devout Catholic couples. Indeed, other loving interactions between them can be expressions of the virtue of chastity which can provide God's grace to temper their bodily appetites and protect their marriage from selfishness, aggressiveness, and lust. Chastity is not simply repression of sexual desire. It can be an expression of the purity and holiness expressed by the married couple linking their sexuality to God himself who is all holiness. Chastity's connection to the Creator elevates sex from mere animal instinct and pleasure-seeking to the ultimate gift of creation of a human soul when the couple is open to that gift as they fully and unselfishly express their mutual love.

In contrast to those who wish to avoid conception, couples who desire to conceive may also take advantage of fertility awareness for the purpose of conceiving a child. Either is in accord with natural design by God.

In the aggregate, most Christian and non-Christian religions of the world place the responsibility of when and if to have children on the married couple. They cannot know whether their choice is in keeping with the holy will of God. Indeed, in many or even most instances they do not know whether their sexual intimacy is in direct conflict with the Creator. Moreover, the means they take to prevent pregnancy may be physically or spiritually harmful to them. When it is also considered that oral contraceptives may be and intrauterine devices are abortifacients, a whole new level of immorality is introduced. To atheist and non-religious couples one might think any form of contraception is acceptable unless they believe that human life has at least the value of the lower animals many so vociferously defend. When it begins they are unable to say, regardless of their strong opinions.

The teachings of the Catholic Church regarding human sexuality neither directly endanger human life nor the relationship of the married couple to Almighty God. While they can certainly offend him in the way they relate to each other or to their children, those who desire to be holy because he is holy can get their married life off to the best start possible and keep it that way.

Little Black Lives Do
They Matter?

John F. Fisher MD

*Originally published in *Catholic Insight Magazine*, October 23, 2020

Anyone who believes that God is the Author of all life and loves us unconditionally (and many who don't) would instinctively endorse the notion that black lives do *indeed* matter. How can we not? Recent events have now persuaded many of us that black lives matter more than others on planet Earth in 2020, especially when star amateur and professional athletes, the media, celebrities, and our politicians talk incessantly about it. This juggernaut of a slogan has made its way to billboards, ball caps, football helmets, and even tattoo parlors and must be accepted as an obvious truth by all. The punishment for any dissent is being labeled with the dreaded "R" word. Many of us who would ordinarily be sympathetic to such a humanitarian cause have also found it on boarded up restaurants, corner grocery broken windows, looted department store doors, federal building facades, burning police cars, and historic monuments. Such wanton destruction and taking from others causes us to doubt our initial instincts especially when it is appreciated that the founders of the movement admit to being "trained Marxists." Can a slogan symbolize both good and evil simultaneously? Not likely if it is intrinsically good in its meaning.

How about the littlest black lives, the ones in the womb? Do they matter? One would wonder, since black women are five times more likely to have an abortion than white women. In 2016, of the 546,091 legal abortions performed, 137,510 involved black babies. That 25% is the highest among any other ethnic group. The very next year, the CDC reported that there were 335,667 black deaths from all other causes. If the percentages have not dramatically changed in one year, *that would make abortion the leading cause of death among black people.*

The origins of such an egregious reality can be traced to Margaret Sanger, born in 1875 rather ironically to Irish Catholic parents. In 1921, Sanger founded The American Birth Control League, which became Planned Parenthood. Her infamous Negro Project of 1939, enlisted African American leaders to promote birth control among blacks as family planning. In reality, said Arnold Culbreath, a pro-life African-American pastor of the Peoples Church in Cincinnati, she was promoting eugenics and selective reproduction. That black people were among her main targets was made patently obvious by a speech she gave on birth control to a women's auxiliary branch of the Ku Klux Klan. In the buildup to World War II, she praised Nazi eugenic efforts and expressed contempt for "those elements at large in the population whose children are a menace to the national health and well-being." Apparently unrepentant even after the war, in a 1957 interview with Mike Wallace, Sanger, as president of the International Planned Parenthood Federation, said that "the greatest sin is bringing children into the world that have disease from their parents and have no chance in the world to be a human being practically. Delinquents. Prisoners. All sorts of things — marked when they're born." Let us pray that faced with death in her final illness from congestive heart failure, she called upon Our Lord to forgive the horrific legacy she left in her wake.

With the matriarchs of black families among the most faithful churchgoers in the U.S., what are they hearing from the pulpits? A new Pew Research Center analysis finds that just 4% of sermons shared on U.S. black church websites in the spring of 2019 discussed abortion even once – and when they did, it was rarely mentioned repeatedly. Still, pastors who broached the topic were nearly unanimous in their opposition. Perhaps the young adults are not going to church to hear these opinions about abortion. Nevertheless, they *are* praying. Indeed, a survey, which was conducted in 2017, sampled the views of U.S. Protestant adults between the ages of 23 and 30. It found that 72 percent of African-American young adults said they spend regular time in private prayer, compared to 58 percent of white young adults. Forty-seven percent of black young adults said they regularly read the Bible privately, compared to 33 percent of white young adults. So, it appears that blacks are far more religious than whites. "What are they praying for?" it might be asked. The evangelical research group, Barna, tells us that the needs of family, guidance in crisis, thanksgiving, and asking for forgiveness are the most popular subjects. These data suggest that the majority of black young adults are religious people.

Unfathomably, these same black people largely identify themselves as Democrats one of whose major party platforms condones abortion at any stage in gestation. 'Thou shalt not kill' has to be one subject that these religious people have not given any serious thought to. They should; because if the major Democrat politicians genuinely believe in their hearts that abortion is not evil, it follows that blacks should not trust anything they say. *Period.* The upcoming U.S. election for president should tell us what percentage of blacks have drunk the Democrat 'kool-ade.'

Many religious people have referred to the Democrat party as the party of death as did Father Ed Meeks, pastor of Christ the King Catholic Church in Towson, MD who called Catholic Joe Biden their standard bearer in a recent homily. He further told his congregation that there are three non-negotiables for Catholics with regard to voting: sanctity of life, sanctity of marriage, and religious liberty. He said, "Joe Biden is unabashedly pro-abortion…who supports abortion for any reason or for no reason right up to and even beyond the moment of birth." "Joe Biden opposes the church's teaching on the sanctity of marriage." "While he was vice-president, he publicly endorsed same-sex marriage… And in 2016, while still vice-president, he officiated over the 'wedding' ceremony of two men."

This is the leader that the majority of black people apparently will choose for their president. Once again, all pro-life, religious people must pray for Mr. Biden and his party. Their souls are in serious jeopardy. We must also pray for pregnant black women, no matter what circumstance they find themselves in, that they will ask the Good Lord for guidance and bring into the world those little black lives that matter.

The Universal Quest for Affection

Looking for Love in Some of the Wrong Places

John F. Fisher, MD

*Originally published in *Catholic Insight Magazine* April 28, 2022

It probably begins *in utero* when hearing awareness first develops. The baby inside, safe and wet and warm, hears the noises of activity nearby, but at first they are just sounds. Later they may register as soothing or frightening depending on the goings on outside. The squeezing pressure of the uterus at delivery and the chaos in the delivery room must be bewildering and scary. The newborn has to be terrified gasping for air, hearing its own voice, and feeling it vibrating inside for the first time while freezing cold. Having no language, there's little else to do except holler. Finally, being held close to mother's chest must feel a little soothing until being snatched away for the first bath. Terror and the hollering returns.

It isn't long before the newborn makes fuzzy eye contact with mom and begins imprinting with her. When vision clears up, the bond increases and baby begins to crave her warm caresses and kisses. Soon that feeling and sense of belonging likely extends to others in the family especially when they demonstrate their love with reassuring smiles and playful gestures and touches. In a healthy family, love for mom and dad and brothers and sisters flourishes for life. If the newborn is a boy, affection is shown to him in masculine terms like "That's my big boy" or "Look at my little buddy" or "Come 'ere, Pal, let me hold you." For girls, the tone is different: "There's my little sweetie pie" or "She's so sweet" or "That's Daddy's little angel." Gender identification begins early.

Testosterone is one of the principal hormones whose effect on boys' brains helps determine some of their behaviors as toddlers, young children, adolescents, and adult men which distinguishes them from their female counterparts (Hines, M. Human gender development. Neurosis Biobehav Rev 2020; 118:89-96). Socialization also influences gender identity. For example, parents, other children, and teachers encourage kids to play with toys which are considered gender- appropriate. Once they know they are girls or boys they tend to imitate the behavior and model the object and play choices of their own gender more than that of opposite gender in the course of their childhood.

Gender identity is obviously complicated and multifactorial. Nevertheless, most people who have male-typical external genitalia think of themselves as boys or men and most people who have female- typical external genitalia do not. Moreover, their childhood reflects these self-images. Along with that development comes the strong yearning to fit in—to be liked by someone. There is a natural attraction for others who share the same interests and even more for those who are talented or popular. These feelings are the rudiments of affection and more. A very healthy kind of bond develops among boys and men who are able to share their ideas and dreams, find a similar sense of humor, laugh at life's circumstances, and join in the same activities. For girls and women, it's likely identical, but I won't presume to speak for them. A few of these relationships become lifelong friendships.

The sometimes-vocal minority who dispute their anatomic gender assignment are considered to have gender dysphoria and are convinced it occurred *in utero* or before. Because many come from families which would be considered dysfunctional, the truth of that opinion is far from settled and continues to be the subject of genetic, sociologic, and neurologic research. Nevertheless, these individuals, too, have a normal desire to fit in and there is no reason to believe that they cannot bond with others of like mind and develop lifelong affection for them.

Children are naturally curious about their own anatomy and that of persons of the same or opposite gender and are likely to compare and contrast openly or surreptitiously. Reprimands from parents or surrogates and older siblings for fondling themselves or purposeful, mischievous leering at others' private parts establish in them certain norms of behavior as right or wrong, but it is doubtful if most children are capable of actual sin. As they begin to participate in various family faith traditions during their elementary school years, foundational morality develops.

What is considered immoral varies widely among churches, synagogues, mosques, and temples and their representative private schools. Such mores can be stringently or leniently reinforced by parental figures. At home, a growing child is likely to feel most secure and safe if the natural affection they have for mom and dad is returned without strings attached. Thankfully, most parents have unconditional love for their children and show it daily. However, some children are not exposed to any faith traditions and are raised by parents whose priorities are elsewhere. As a result, the lines between perceptions of good and evil are extremely blurred and the search for affection from *someone* never wanes.

The surge of adolescent hormones brings with it striking changes in anatomy, sexual fantasies, morning erections, and nocturnal emissions. Self-exploration leads to unprecedented, pleasurable moments and yearnings to repeat them in secret and to cautiously joke about these actions to classmates and friends. Although both parents had the same experiences years ago, embarrassment prevents most of them from broaching these subjects with their children. The majority are content with leaving questions about the biology to educators and the morality to religious leaders. However, the personal views of both teachers and preachers are widely disparate and also tempered by their own experiences.

Given the thousands of religious denominations, it may be worthwhile to examine the oldest Christian religion because it has clearly-articulated beliefs about the human sex drive. It is probable that some may view the teachings of the Catholic Church with regard to sexuality as far too extreme and prohibitive. Nevertheless, they originate from the Church's definition of chastity referred to as a virtue characterized by the successful integration of a person's sexuality into who they are-- bodily and spiritually (CCC 2337). Anatomically, the purpose is obvious. According to Catholicism, when it is used as a complete and lifelong gift of love and the possible procreation of new life between a man and a woman and God, that purpose brings genuine integrity to the married couple and not mere physical pleasure and release. Indeed, it is impossible for God who *is* love (1 Jn 4:16) to be connected with any act which is not loving and holy. The marital act ideally then will foster that loving relationship to God. It is therefore absurd that casual or group sex, pleasuring oneself, rape, bestiality, or incest-- by either gender, designated or desired, would fit easily into God's loving use for our genitalia.

Be that as it may, an orgasmic climax is among life's most powerful sensations and its unique pleasure is indelibly written into the human memory. Understandably, the desire to experience it repeatedly in many forms or sometimes *any* form is strong, especially among young people. Older persons, too, can easily recall and ruminate about the intimate encounters of long ago. Moreover, for young and old, innumerable sources of arousal are part of our daily experience on television, the movies, smart phones, and the internet. Attractive people can hardly be avoided in any walk-of-life and it takes effort not to fantasize about them, especially when they purposely flaunt their good looks.

God has anticipated our need to resist a life of dissipation, and offers us that grace-giving gift of chastity. A chaste life has its foundation in the waters of Baptism in which the Holy Spirit calls all to imitate the purity of Christ (CCC 2345). This virtue does not develop immediately for hardly any of us. We who desire to seek it, often find it a difficult and lifelong pursuit as we learn to master ourselves and govern our passions. Accordingly, failings in the realm of chastity must be among the most frequent admissions priests hear in the confessional whether from the laity or even from other priests. Success or genuine progress brings with it the blessing of a healthy, inner peace.

We who completely reject God's assistance or are agnostics or atheists are unlikely to be able to rein in our desires and are destined for a life of chaos and unhappiness for ourselves and our families. However, most of us were raised in religious traditions. Even if we have strayed from those spiritual roots, there likely will remain a nagging deep inside which tells us that when we have used another person of the same or opposite gender primarily for sexual gratification, we have wronged ourselves, wronged the other person, and if we still believe, offended God. If that were not intrinsically evil, why would we hide the prurient details from those we love? Why would we bother to confess them to a priest? Why would some of us so vehemently and vociferously argue for various forms of sexual release as normal variants? With apologies to Shakespeare, "The ladies (*and the gentlemen*) protest too much, methinks." At a minimum, our actions have been beneath our dignity as a human.

The reality remains that 7.1% of people in the U.S. identify as not heterosexual. In fact, one in five in generation Z (adults born after 1997) identify as LGBT with bisexual being most common (Gallup). The absence of proof notwithstanding, most would claim they were born that way. According to a 2020 report from the Williams Institute of UCLA Law School, half of them consider themselves religious. It can be cautiously assumed that religious people like these continue to believe they are called to "love the Lord your God with all your heart, all your soul, all your mind, and all your strength and love your neighbor as yourself…" (Mark 12:30-31). One might ask those believers whether the orgasmic pleasure derived from same-gender or bisexual sexual intercourse can possibly be an expression of that love for God and love of neighbor and whether chastity in those relationships is even possible.

It might be argued that a loving relationship without sexual intimacy between a same-gender, religious couple can be chaste. That form of affection would be analogous to best friends who are roommates. In contrast, what about openly gay people who exchange vows in religious services who thereafter pleasure one another in sundry ways? How would those couples compare their union to that of a religious man and woman married by a rabbi, mullah, minister, or a priest? Would God accept as holy any and all ceremonies asking for his witness because he does not discriminate?

I won't attempt to convince those who are certain there is no God or are disinterested agnostics. Sexual gratification to them among consenting adults is limited only by their imagination. Such activity can provide the superficial and short-lived, physical pretense of affection.

Usually focused on our families and friends, we can and should save some room in our prayer life for our troubled, gender- dysphoric brothers and sisters and pray that they will find God and love in all the right places before they "face their final curtain." Believers or not, He loves them with the same intensity that He loves each of us and *that* kind of affection comes with available, overabundant grace. Few of them realize that the grace to seek him was implanted before they were conceived. "Before I formed you in the womb, I knew you." (Jer 1:5). It is even more certain than their gender at birth. But God has given us free will and will provide all the evidence and grace we need to believe and to master our desires to please him, but he will not force us. May that freely given gift not be labeled by any of us, "Return to Sender."

Where Are You Going, My Little One, Little One?

John F. Fisher MD

*Originally published in *Catholic Insight Magazine* June 7, 2023 as *"God, Atheism, and Becoming Like Little Children"*

Amen, I say to you, unless you turn and become like children, you will not enter the kingdom of heaven (Mt 18:3).

Though many of Jesus's words might be subject to interpretation in various faith traditions, Matthew's report of what he said in Galilee in response to the question, "Who is the greatest in the Kingdom of Heaven?" seems pretty direct. Yet, most of the turning and becoming in our world today is in the adult direction. What is it about children which could possibly allow their entry before the rest of us? After all, they depend on us mature people for their education, safety, and very existence. We certainly don't need a four-year-old to show us anything—do we?

It took a 40-year-old Edwin Hubble with his telescope in the first part of the 20th Century to prove that our universe is ever expanding and 28-year-old Stephen Hawking and 34-year-old Roger Penrose provided strong evidence our stars and planets have not always been there. Ernst Ruska invented the electron microscope in 1933 at age 27 and modern instruments can now magnify human cells a million times and have revealed them to be ordered universes in themselves. These are the works of mature minds. It is certainly not child's play.

Yet, ponder: It is not surprising that most of the scientists making landmark observations today have become atheists, agnostics, or are no longer especially interested in the hereafter despite growing up in religious families. Their scientific method has become their god and is bound to eventually show that the idea of a loving, omnipotent being creating all of this out of nothing is preposterous, wishful thinking. The more they discover, the more arrogant they become. Drawn like moths to a flame, they bask in their recognition at national and international scientific meetings. Acolytes from the major secular universities supporting their research fawn all over them because of their brilliance and the media are quick to follow suit. Consequently, their conclusions about creation become quite contagious for the rest of us. We figure that they must be right and assume that our scientists will get us the evidence that there's nobody out there before we die.

There is at least some pull in the opposite direction since many of us grownups love our kids more than life itself. Many of us are still in the habit of going home to our families, reading a story to our moppets at bedtime, and tucking them in with, "Now I lay me down to sleep…" like our parents did with us. We might even tell them about a kindly father in heaven who made us, made the earth, and all the animals and plants just because he loves us. Of course, they trust whatever we tell them and innocently and instinctively believe it.

Nevertheless, our collective genius has evolved us far beyond Santa Claus, Tinker Toys, and Legos and we're not going back! What we have failed to consider is that brighter minds than ours have been trying to prove that God is a myth since humans inhabited the planet and that the argument for or against is unlikely to be settled in our own lifetime. That's going to leave some of the scientists and us at least a tiny bit uneasy when we keep remembering back to our own childhood and what our parents and Sunday-school teachers told us. That nagging little voice will always be asking, "What if I'm wrong and reject God in the short time I have left? Will he reject me? As has been said, "There are no atheists in foxholes."

Lest we think that modern geniuses have all the answers, with none of the tools we have today, Thomas Aquinas, using his prodigious intellect alone, proved 700 years ago that the universe has not always existed and that there has to have been an Unmoved Mover (perhaps the one who ignited the Big Bang?). Thomas himself, undoubtedly familiar with Matthew 18:3, had some insightful observations about small children. He tells us that little children are not pretentious and do not put on airs. They are simply themselves. They are pure and not dominated by unchaste desires like many of us mature folks. Rather than manipulative like so many adults, they are true friends who do not hold grudges and forget wrongs quickly. They are happy to overlook the morning's scuffles in order to play again in the afternoon. Their limited rational powers at so young an age prevent them from real sin. Ironically, despite his remarkable intellect, the purity of Aquinas's own heart was such that, on the testimony of Reginald, his confessor, his general confession before dying was like that of a child of five. Had he been remembering Matthew 18:3?

Those of us who call ourselves believers can be just as arrogant as the rocket scientists. These superior intellects of ours have made some of us so-called scripture scholars, fluent in Greek, Aramaic, and Hebrew positive how every passage should be interpreted. We grownups believe we know who God is and how He wants to be worshiped, don't we? After all, we're the ones who designed Notre Dame and Chartres. We have the knowledge to compose hymns that bring a tear to the eye in their simplicity or exhilaration in their incredible vocal or symphonic harmonies and mathematical complexity. Why should we turn the clock back to enter God's kingdom when we have many more advanced resources for sanctification than a child? What is it that little kids have that we have left behind?

The most obvious is their innocence. Indeed, innocent trust is one of the basic attributes of being a child. When we tell them there is a Santa Claus who's kind and jolly and will bring them gifts on Christmas, they write letters to him and address them to the North Pole. When we take them to church or Sunday school and they are told that they have a Father in heaven who made them, they accept it immediately and without question. The prayers they say and the songs they sing with that knowledge are not only precious to us, but likely to Him as well. About the worst thing a four-year-old can do is to stop up the toilet with half–a–roll of toilet paper. Sadly, it doesn't take long before, as high school kids, they can take those same rolls and stream them over the house of someone they don't like out of pure malice. A four-year-old white boy can sit with a black boy and make vroom sounds happily together with toy trucks and be totally unconcerned that their skins are a different shade. Little children in their simplicity are fascinated with puppies and delighted if the puppy licks the chocolate off their entire faces. Some angry adults purposely teach puppies to become attack dogs in some kind of warped machismo to menace or even kill others if necessary. As Aquinas indicated, a child can be momentarily annoyed when another kid pushes him down and in half–a–tick scamper after him and tag him "it" laughing uproariously in playful forgiveness. Some "grown-ups" will shoot to kill for less. Harboring a grudge never occurs to a child, but many of us older folks have carried around several for years for what we consider personal slights of us, our families, our politics, our research, or our religion. Some of us have even killed or maimed innocent people because we're so sure ours is the true faith. Tragically in these matters, too, kids believe everything we tell them.

If there is an all-knowing Creator of the Universe, we adults can't be more than infinitesimally advanced than our three-year-olds to Him. He must be amused by the ideas of our greatest scientists and mathematicians, but lovingly allows us to pontificate at national meetings, and win the accolades of our colleagues or even Nobel prizes for our "landmark" discoveries. We are even allowed to use our "great" intellects to turn away from Him and teach others that He is an invention of our fear of death and the unknown. Even though each of us instinctively knows good from evil, we are free to hurt others in so many disparate and sometimes violent ways. We can selfishly amass great wealth and power for ourselves and families without a thought to the huddled masses around us. Our kids instinctively love and believe in us. They are proud to copy everything we do. God is not in the forcing business. He gave us the beautiful gift of free will. If He does love us as we were taught, He wouldn't totally abandon us as puffed up as we might become. Jesus repeatedly confronted the scribes and Pharisees whom He loved with the truth about their arrogance and hypocrisy and won some of them over with his teaching and example. What He offered free for the asking was the gift of faith. Faith is not something which the intelligentsia of our world think they can reason to or reject. Belief is free for the asking from Him. So, if the astrophysicists and we are in our right minds, we might be humble enough to admit that we can't know absolutely about the creation of the universe. The safest fallback posture for any of us who remain uncertain to adopt could then be, "If you're out there, Lord, please help my unbelief." A loving Creator would not likely say, "No" to His creature for such a humble request before death. Following that freely given gift, we will all, hopefully, have time for our own search for childlike innocence.

The title, 'Where Are You Going, My Little One, Little One'? is a line from a thought-provoking song written by Harry Belafonte, Malvina

Reynolds, and Alan Greene, entitled "Turn Around." There is an obvious answer to this question for innocent children whether taken from us gradually by disease, suddenly in an accident, or deliberately in traumatic abuse or abortion: "This day you will be with me in Paradise."

The Rocky Road from Doubt to Faith

John F. Fisher, MD

Originally published in Catholic Insight Magazine, August 16, 2023

Thanks to my Irish Catholic mother and 12 years with the good sisters of six parochial schools and four more years at the University of Notre Dame, I am *not* among the 10% in this country who are atheists. Many non-believers who have made a serious effort to consider whether God exists would write me off as brainwashed. Not so fast, brothers and sisters.

Time and again in the course of my religious and secular education, the subjects of where we came from, where we are going, and who Jesus of Nazareth is (or was) have come up and I have had to take a hard look at them either formally or informally. With my background, escape was not possible. I finally came to realize that the veritable immersion in these subjects has been my great fortune. I have been repeatedly forced to deal with, arguably, the most important issues any thinking human can face in their life on earth. If God does not exist, our time on this planet is ours to use fruitfully or completely waste. On the other hand, if there is a God with a grand design for his creatures, failure to consider how each of us might fit into that plan could spell our own doom.

My frequent exposure to these subjects and quiet contemplation about them has made me realize that God's existence (or not) cannot be absolutely proven with facts. Sadly, without them, thoughtful atheists refuse to believe. These doubting Thomases want the supernatural being to make some kind of a dramatic appearance in their lives. What they don't realize is, that if that occurred, their free will would be suddenly swept from them and they would be forced like robots to believe. It makes no sense that a loving God would desire the love of creatures who have no choice in the matter. But over the centuries, perhaps there are colossal hints.

Accordingly, the purpose of this essay is to strengthen the faith of those who believe (my own included), to challenge atheists who are simply interested in the subject or passionate in their unbelief, and to awaken the consciousness of lukewarm agnostics. If there is a God, can there be any more important topic?

It seems reasonable to begin the strengthening, challenging, and awakening process with the purported existence of a Supreme Being. Scientists believe that the universe was formed some 13.7 billion years ago with the release of unmeasurable energy colloquially known as the Big Bang; but what or who set off the Big Bang? There are many theories. Take for example, the argument from motion. In the 13th Century, Thomas Aquinas reasoned that all things we observe have been placed in motion and that no thing has placed itself in motion. He assumed that if something is in motion, it has to be caused *to be in motion* by another thing. He concluded that there is not an infinite chain of events causing things to be in motion. If that were true, we would never observe something moving because the original cause would have taken an infinite time to set in motion the moving thing we observe. Since there is motion, the cause-and-effect chain must have a beginning. He deduced from this that there must be a First Cause. While St. Thomas believed in a Supreme Being as the First Cause, his reasoning certainly does not establish this as fact.

A counter theory is that *it is the universe which has always existed* as energy and will continue to exist going through a never- ending cycle of expansion and contraction and then expansion (Big Bang) over and over. This provocative argument likewise has not been established as fact. Many atheists who subscribe to this theory assume this proves that there is no Supreme Being. On the contrary, it is a violation of logic and a fallacy in thinking that if an argument cannot prove the existence of God, it means that there is no God. A more logical approach for an atheist-scientist would be to consider the existence of a Supreme Being as possible, but cannot be proven. If he or she were raised in the Catholic Church, they should have been taught that while there may be compelling evidence for a Creator, the faith which convinces and motivates is a gift and not something that can always be reasoned to (Eph. 2:8; Phil 1:29). That should lead to a safer fallback position for the doubting scientist such as, "If you are out there, God, help my unbelief." Those of us who are believers would expect that our God could not refuse to grant the gift of faith to such an earnest and humble request.

However, blind faith simply because of the possibility of an intelligent creator would not satisfy most of us either. What tangible evidence is supportive of the existence of God? Let's begin with the order in the universe. Even an uneducated person would be astounded by taking the time to look closely at the world around us. The smallest animals who creep on the ground, inhabit the seas, lakes, and rivers are amazingly complex life forms which follow set patterns of existence. Indeed, one living cell is a universe of its own and functions in an incredibly ordered fashion within and near surrounding cells and their products. Those of us who have studied the physical sciences can't help but recognize the laws obeyed by the countless stars and their galaxies and the planets which orbit around them. Atheists would make the argument that the order in nature is adequately explained by the laws of physics and chance. They might point out two examples of this in the way that crystals form and the way the solar system formed. However, they might have overlooked the fact that the very laws of physics are part of the very order they try to explain away. Interestingly, it is now known that Newton's laws of gravity and mechanics are not quite exact. Laws discovered by Einstein in the 20th Century reveal that Newton's laws were reasonable approximations. Unexpectedly, Einstein's theory of relativity and gravity reveal an order that is even more wonderful and profound.

The late Henry Morris, erstwhile chair of the Department of Civil Engineering at Virginia Polytechnic Institute, who earned a PhD in hydraulic engineering and was a noted creation-scientist took a mathematical look at the argument that chance explained the order we observe in our universe. This opinion is held by many non-believers. Demonstrating the superficial reasoning of such a position, Dr. Morris noted that entirely random processes generate *disorder and confusion*; simplicity rather than the complexity we see about us. He gave the example of a series of ten flash cards, numbered from one to ten, thoroughly and randomly mixed. If these cards are then laid out successively in a row along the table, it would be extremely unlikely that the numbers would fall out in order from one to ten. Multiplying together all the numbers from one to ten, he calculated that the probability of a progressively ordered arrangement of flash cards is only one in 3,628,800.

A conversation at a nearby tavern among graduates of Cal Tech, but hopefully not Notre Dame, might deteriorate into the almost universally debunked Monkey Theorem after a few pints. The most popular version poses the mathematical question of whether an infinite number of monkeys given an infinite number of typewriters and infinite time could type out all the works of Shakespeare without a misspelled word or a missing space. One statistician calculated the ridiculous chance of 1 in 26^{20} of even typing the first 20 letters of Hamlet correctly! An obvious question remains for skeptics: Could the order in our universe be explained instead by an incredibly intelligent being?

Assuming that readers have not found something more interesting or important to do and are at least still open to further discussion of things that are beyond the scope of normal scientific understanding, the events described in the writings of Moses and the prophets should be addressed. To date, no remnants of the ark built by Noah (Gn. 6:14) have been found on Mount Ararat in Turkey. Egyptian papyruses do indicate the presence of semitic slaves, many of whom were expelled from that country, but definitive proof of expulsion related to their worship of Yaweh, let alone the aftermath following the sprinkling of lamb's blood on doorway lintels (Ex. 12:7) is lacking. In addition, no certified Egyptian chariot wheels, armor, or human bones have been recovered in or near the Red Sea. Notwithstanding the excitement in the classic action film with Harrison Ford in *Raiders of the Lost Ark*, the Ark of the Covenant containing Aaron's staff, manna, and the tablets brought down by Moses from Mount Sinai no longer exists and cannot be proven to have ever existed. Nevertheless, the zeal of the estimated 28 generations of the Israelites from Abraham to the birth of Jesus of Nazareth and the motivation of modern religious Jews since then must have been spawned by at least *some* astonishing events even if they cannot be proved.

That Jesus existed is an historical fact apart from scripture. The evidence is both long-established and widespread. Within a few decades of his supposed lifetime, he is mentioned by Jewish and Roman historians, as well as by dozens of Christian writings. The gospels of Matthew, Mark, and Luke written in different times and languages are remarkably synchronous.

C. S. Lewis popularized the argument that Jesus was either a liar or a lunatic or the Lord: "A man who was merely a man and said the sort of things Jesus said would not be simply a great moral teacher. He would either be a lunatic—on the level with the man who says he is a poached egg—or else he would be the Devil of Hell. You must make your choice. Either this man was, and is, the Son of God, or else a madman or something worse [...] Now it seems to me obvious that He was neither a lunatic nor a fiend: and consequently, however strange or terrifying or unlikely it may seem, I have to accept the view that He was and is God." (Mere Christianity, 55-56).

The impact of Jesus on the ancient world and the one we live in has been duplicated by no one else in history. Historian Philip Schaff described this overwhelming influence which Jesus had on the subsequent history and cultures of the world: "This Jesus of Nazareth, without money and arms, conquered more millions than Alexander, Caesar, Mohammed, and Napoleon; without science [...] he shed more light on things human and divine than all philosophers and scholars combined; without the eloquence of schools, he spoke such words of life as were never spoken before or since, and produced effects which lie beyond the reach of orator or poet; without writing a single line, he set more pens in motion, and furnished themes for more sermons, orations, discussions, learned volumes, works of art, and songs of praise than the whole army of great men of ancient and modern times."

Logically, how could a simple carpenter's son accomplish all this without the press, the internet, money, connections to famous people, or coercion of anyone? People who interacted with him must have seen some astounding things like turning water into wine, immediate cleansing of some chronic skin diseases at least resembling leprosy, healing a paralyzed man, restoring a deformed hand, bringing sight to a person born blind, and raising three people from the dead including Lazarus who had been in the tomb for four days. There were apparently countless others than those described in detail in Scripture. However, raising himself from the dead after an unquestionably cruel torture and crucifixion *would trump everything*. There are too many feats like these to explain them away as slight-of-hand, exaggerations, false reports, or manufactured conspiracies by a few malevolent followers. Why would these "conspirators" travel throughout the known world afterward and willingly suffer persecution and death as martyrs to the cause of a dead "moral teacher"? Wouldn't even *one* of them be expected to defect? Countless others, not from his time, suffered unthinkable tortures and death for the love of Jesus. Yet some of the most learned men and women of today dismiss this Jesus out of hand! Their lack of even a *little curiosity* is unfathomable.

It is now appropriate to examine any evidence that Jesus actually *did* rise from the dead. For this, we shall turn to the Shroud of Turino, Italy. Some believe this burial cloth is a witness to the resurrection and some think it is a medieval fraud. The cloth itself was subjected to scientific analysis in the 1980s. Evidence reveals that it is a high-quality, linen cloth with blood on it as well as an image of a naked, apparently crucified man with scourge marks front and back. The image shows neither the thumbs nor ears of the man. Unexpectedly, there is dried blood from nail marks apparently emanating from wrists and ankles. Although many paintings of the crucifixion of Jesus depict nails driven through the hands, his body weight on a cross could not have been supported by nails in those places. Spikes through the wrists and ankles could have supported him and the image is consistent with those findings. In addition, such major trauma to the median nerves would cause the thumbs to contract behind the hands which could explain why they are not visible.

Since the Catholic Church is unafraid of and interested in the truth, scientists from the U.S. were the first group permitted by the Vatican to closely examine the shroud—38 agnostics, 3 raised as Catholics, 34 Protestants, 3 raised Jewish. They were experts from the disciplines of nuclear physics, chemistry, radiology, botany, history, textiles, medicine, mathematics, archeology, forensic pathology, photography, and geology. Thus, the shroud was examined from all these aspects. All arrived in Turino to scrutinize the shroud and all thought the shroud was a fake. All departed Turino concluding the shroud is *not* a fake, but unable to explain how the image got on that old linen cloth. Three types of pollen found only in Israel were present on this linen. The dried blood of the crucified victim was determined to be AB +, the universal receiver, and DNA was found containing both X and Y chromosomes. There was also evidence that the blood was from a tortured human, not only with indications of flogging, but because the blood had a high bilirubin content consistent with significant hemolysis. Inexplicably, the image shows areas of the body where there was no contact by the cloth. The expert panel concluded that the image is not a painting, not a drawing, not a rubbing, not a scorching from a hot statue, and not a photograph.

Carbon-dating initially determined that the shroud originated between 1260 and 1390. This disappointing finding led to the conclusion that the shroud had to be an obvious fraud from the middle ages. Not surprisingly, research stopped. However, it has been subsequently found that cotton cloth repairs to the shroud following fire damage from that era likely "contaminated" the linen in the carbon-dating process leaving its age still open to further investigation. A current theory holds that the image was created by some type of radiation. Many Catholics and other Christians believe that a burst of energy might well have been given off to produce the image at the moment of the resurrection of this man perhaps explaining why it is present in areas not in contact with the shroud.

In the end, whether the burial cloth is that of Jesus of Nazareth and is authentic remains an open-ended question. Science is not currently able to prove it. However, based on the evidence, it seems highly improbable that the shroud is a painting or somehow artificially produced. The investigators left the question open so that those who wish to believe it is authentic are not hindered by scientific objection. On the other hand, without absolute proof, those who favor the opinion that the shroud is not authentic are also free to do so in light of presently available data (1). Could the shroud be our only physical hint that Jesus' resurrection actually occurred? At the very least, it might be "food for (atheist's) thought".

It is common knowledge among Christians of many denominations that the Catholic Church teaches that a priest, employing the Passover words of Jesus at the Last Supper during Mass, invokes the Holy Spirit to bring about a "transubstantiation" in the unleavened bread and the wine. Without a change in appearance, these ordinary "works of human hands" and "fruit of the vine" according to Catholic belief *actually and tangibly* become the body and blood of Jesus Himself. Few non-Catholic Christians realize that this rite originated in the first century. Despite this, some Catholics themselves have struggled with this teaching and a recent Pew survey indicated that less than 40% of Catholics actually believe in the Real Presence. On occasion, even priests themselves have struggled with doubts about transubstantiation. One rather fantastic example occurred in Lanciano, Italy in 750. In the little church of St. Legontian, a priest had been having these Real-Presence doubts. Reportedly, after reciting the words of consecration at Mass, the host (the unleavened bread) inexplicably and suddenly became live flesh and the wine became blood which coagulated into several globules. The flesh and the coagulated blood were placed in a marble tabernacle above the altar for permanent adoration. In the 1970s and again in 1981, Professors Odoardo Linoli and Ruggero Bertelli were permitted to conduct scientific analyses of the still incredibly-well-preserved flesh and blood taking photomicrographs. They concluded that the flesh is human flesh, astoundingly cardiac muscle, and the clotted blood is also human blood type AB +, as found in the Shroud of Turino. The preservation of these human substances exposed to the atmosphere for almost 1400 years remains unexplained.

A more contemporary example with some similarity to the purportedly miraculous occurrence in Lanciano took place in Buenos Aires, Argentina in the church of Santa Maria y Caballito Almagro in 1996. On August 18th after Mass, a parishioner informed the parish priest, Father Alejandro Pezet, that a consecrated host had been desecrated by placing it on a candleholder in the back of the church. The priest, following the instructions of the Church in such circumstances, put the host in a container filled with water and kept it in the tabernacle waiting for the host to dissolve and planning on disposing of it after it no longer had the appearance of bread. To his astonishment, the priest found that the bread had not dissolved at all, but transformed into a piece of bloody tissue greater in size than the original wafer of bread. The parish priests hurriedly went to the Archbishop of Buenos Aires, Cardinal Jorge Mario Bergoglio (now Pope Francis), to tell him what had happened. It was decided that the host should be kept in the tabernacle without publicizing its origin. Three years later, the bloody tissue had *still* not decomposed, even though no special attempt was made to preserve it. The archbishop decided to have it scientifically examined in the presence of one of the church's representatives, scientist Dr. Ricardo C. Gomez. So as not to prejudice the investigation, Dr. Gomez took a sample of the bloody fragment and sent it to New York for analysis without revealing its source. A team of five scientists including a forensic pathologist, Dr. Frederic Zugibe of Columbia University. Dr. Zugibe testified that the material is a fragment of cardiac muscle from the left ventricle. Moreover, the heart muscle was found to be in an inflammatory condition because it contained a large number of white blood cells. Since white blood cells die outside a living organism, this indicates that the heart was alive at the time the sample was taken. These white blood cells had penetrated the cardiac tissue, suggesting that the heart had been under severe stress, as if the owner had been beaten severely about the chest. The doctor was then told that the source of the sample was a consecrated host which had first been kept in ordinary water for a month and then for another three years in a container of distilled water. Only then had the sample been taken for analysis. Dr. Zugibe was at a loss to account for this fact. There was no way of explaining it scientifically, he stated. The blood type of the sample once again came from the AB blood group. The sample was sent for genetic testing and it is human DNA from blood type AB, but in contrast to other samples of human DNA used for forensic analysis, no genetic profile of the person from whom the sample came could be demonstrated. Scientific study of the tissue DNA continues at the present time.

So, it appears that a sample of complex human life has emerged from what was made from unleavened bread and water (the host). This in direct contrast to Darwin's theory of evolution which is believed by the greatest scientific minds of the last three centuries— that all life emerged from a single cell which was capable of self- replicating. These cells according to Darwin, subjected to climatic conditions on this planet over billions of years, were capable of explaining *all life forms which exist*. Darwin himself stated in *Origin of Species* the following:

"If it could be demonstrated that any complex organ existed, which could not possibly have been formed by numerous, successive, slight modifications, my theory would absolutely break down. But I can find no such case." (Charles Darwin, *The Origin of Species*). For both believers and non-believers, this Eucharistic miracle if true, *is such a case* and there are other similar recent examples. Though reticent about his religious views, in 1879 Darwin responded that he had never been an atheist in the sense of denying the existence of a god, and that generally "an Agnostic would be the more correct description of my state of mind." (Darwin Correspondence Project, University of Cambridge). What would Darwin have to say 163 years since that earth-shattering publication?

Notwithstanding the purported miraculous occurrences not only during the life of Jesus, but centuries since, it is reasonable to examine some unexplained events related to his followers. Logically, Jesus' mother, Mary, would be foremost among them. Of over 300 reported apparitions of her (appearances of the Blessed Virgin Mary coming down from heaven to earth) only a handful have been sanctioned by the Vatican. For purposes of our rocky road to belief, I have chosen two. First in this lineup are the two apparitions of Our Lady of Guadalupe. These occurred on December 9th and 12th 1531 to a widower, Juan Diego, in Mexico. She met him on Mount Tepeyacac, instructing him to get the bishop to build a church upon that mountain. To do this, she instructed Juan Diego to go pick a batch of flowers growing unexpectedly in the cold nearby, carry them in his cactus-fiber cloak or tilma, and deliver them to the bishop. When Juan Diego got to the bishop and revealed the flowers, the bishop knew a miracle had taken place. Not only had Juan Diego delivered flowers that were out of season, but his cloak was imprinted with a miraculous image of a young pregnant woman in Aztec garb which is still on display in the Basilica of Santa María de Guadalupe in Mexico City.

On the morning of November 14, 1921, an anti-clerical radical entered the basilica carrying a bouquet of roses. The young man placed the flowers several feet before the tilma, genuflected, then walked away. A few moments later, the bouquet containing 29 sticks of dynamite exploded. All around the image, everything was a scene of destruction. Windows burst, vases crumbled, and the marble altar railing of the church was completely destroyed. A brass crucifix was twisted but amazingly, the image of Our Lady of Guadalupe in the tilma was unscathed. The glass casing in which the tilma hung was perfectly intact. No one in the church was harmed. Numerous scientists and researchers have subjected the tilma to extensive study. In 1977, satellite imaging expert, Dr. Aste Tonsman used infrared photography, along with digital enhancement procedures, to examine the cloak. He and colleagues found that the image shows no sketching or outline drawing that would indicate that an artist had produced a painting there. The exact technique used to create the image remains unknown. In addition, on inspection of the corneas of the woman, a startling discovery of a group of people was made. The size of this scene is incredibly small-- 1/100th of an inch-- something that no artist on this earth could have ever painted. In each eye there is an image of a series of people and objects: an Indian unfurling a tilma before a priest, another young man, a half-naked Indian with his lips open and his hands together, pieces of furniture, a ceiling arch, and other details. This is apparently a re-creation in miniature of the exact moment when Bishop Zumarraga beheld the image of Mary with the scene forever imprinted and recorded in the tilma. In 2009, prominent researcher and physicist Dr. Aldofo Orozco, told participants at an International Marian Congress, that there was simply no scientific explanation for the high-quality preservation of the tilma made from cactus fiber. A cloak woven from the agave or maguey plant should have deteriorated within about 30 years. He said that the remarkable preservation of the image and the cloak of Juan Diego from 478 years ago, "is completely beyond any scientific explanation."

Many doctors and scientists studied the tilma in more detail questioning whether the tilma might miraculously be a *living* fabric. Indeed, one researcher discovered that its temperature maintains a constant 98.6 F degrees. Another placed his stethoscope below the black band at Mary's waist in the image, and heard rhythmic beats at 115 pulses per minute - the same as that of a baby in the maternal womb.

Somewhat later in history, our second Marian apparition occurred in 1858 in the town of Lourdes in southern France to Bernadette Soubirous and became the subject of a 1943 movie in for which Jennifer Jones won the academy award for best actress. Bernadette was 14 years-old, the first child of an extremely poor miller, living in the basement of a dilapidated building. She was known as a virtuous girl, though a dull student. In poor health, she had suffered from asthma from an early age. On February 11th, the Virgin Mary purportedly appeared to Bernadette in a cave above the banks of the Gave River. (A much-revered replica of this grotto one- seventh the size of Bernadette's cave has been on the Notre Dame campus since 1896 and it is likely that someone is praying *for something there now*.) There were 18 apparitions in all, the final one occurring on July 16th. Not surprisingly, Bernadette's initial reports provoked skepticism and her daily visions of "the Lady" brought great crowds of the curious. According to Bernadette, the lady of her visions was a girl of 16 or 17 who wore a white robe with a blue sash. Yellow roses covered her feet and a large rosary was on her right arm. In the vision on March 25th, she reportedly said to Bernadette, "I am the Immaculate Conception." It was only when these words were explained to her that Bernadette came to realize who the lady was.

The lady, Bernadette explained, had instructed her to have a chapel built on the spot of the visions. There, the people were to come to wash and drink of the water of the spring that had welled up from the very spot where Bernadette had been instructed to dig.
Few visions have ever undergone the scrutiny that these appearances

of the virgin were subject to. Untold miracles were reported at the shrine and in the waters of the spring. After thorough investigation, Church authorities confirmed the authenticity of the apparitions in 1862. The Grotto of Lourdes has since become a shrine that receives approximately four million pilgrimages with hundreds of exceptional healings each year. As a result, the Lourdes Medical Bureau was instituted in 1905 to render a judgment that a particular cure was near-instantaneous with no relapses throughout the remainder of life, and, in all other ways, scientifically unexplained. Currently, only seventy cases have been recognized as "miraculous" according to the standards of the Bureau. An example which was witnessed by a Nobel-prize-winning physician is worth recounting. Alexis Carrel was born into in a small town in France in 1873. He attended Mass regularly and was educated in Catholic schools. Unfortunately, by the time he went to college he was an agnostic and completely rejected the Catholic faith. Carrel studied biology and medicine and became a world-famous scientist, developing a way to allow organs to survive outside the body. For his invention of techniques for suturing large blood vessels, he was awarded a Nobel Prize in 1912.

Earlier, in 1902, a physician-friend of Dr. Carrel asked his assistance to help take care of sick patients being transported on a train from Lyon to Lourdes. Carrel did not believe in miracles, but agreed to help his friend, but he was also intrigued about natural causes which might explain the quick healings supposedly taking place at Lourdes.

On the train, he encountered Marie Bailly, whose parents and brother had died of tuberculosis Marie had developed advanced tuberculous peritonitis with a distended abdomen with large, hard masses. Because Bailly was half-conscious, Carrel expected her to pass away quickly, perhaps on the train before arriving at Lourdes. Physician-colleagues on the trip agreed with his assessment.

Upon arrival at Lourdes, Marie was taken to the Grotto, where three pitchers of the spring water were sponged over her distended abdomen. After the first pour, she developed a searing pain which lessened after the second pour, and experienced a pleasant sensation after the third. Her stomach began to flatten on the spot and her pulse returned to normal.

Standing behind Marie, Carrel and other physicians were taking notes as water was poured and he wrote the following: "The enormously distended and very hard abdomen began to flatten and within 30 minutes it had completely disappeared. No discharge whatsoever was observed from the body." Marie then sat up in bed, had a meal without stomach upset, got out of bed on her own, and dressed herself the next day. She returned to Lyon on the train, sitting on the hard benches, and arrived refreshed. Amazed, Carrel remained interested in her psychological and physical condition, and arranged that she be monitored by a psychiatrist and a physician for four months. Marie soon afterward joined the sisters of Charity dedicated to work with the sick and the poor. In what was described as a very strenuous life, she died in 1937 at the age of 58.

When Alex Carrel witnessed this exceedingly rapid and seemingly impossible event, he believed he had seen something like a miracle, but remained skeptical and agnostic. He also wanted to avoid being a medical witness to a miraculous event because he feared that it might ruin his career at the medical faculty at Lyon. Shortly thereafter, he made a public statement in writing suggesting that believers were concluding prematurely that the cure was miraculous and the medical community had not carefully examined the facts before dismissing the event.

As Carrel feared, the fact that he thought it possible that Bailly's cure was miraculous spelled the end of his career at the medical faculty of Lyon. Ironically, this was fortunate for Carrel because he left for the United States to begin research at the University of Chicago and later at Rockefeller University and on to his Nobel Prize.

Carrel returned to Lourdes many times, and on one occasion, witnessed another miraculous cure – the instantaneous return of the sight of an 18-month-old blind boy. He remained doubtful, but was finally received again into the Catholic Church in 1942.

Arguably, Mary, the biological mother of Jesus would be the most important of his followers in this life and the next if there is one. Assuming, as he claimed, that he and the father are one (Jn 10:30), she has to be in constant, intimate contact with the creator of the universe. Miracles associated with her apparitions would not be surprising and even expected. Indeed, no one other that Jesus himself is the focus of more intercessory prayers for the problems on this planet than she. Rosaries by the millions are said daily by Catholics asking her with each click of the beads to "pray for us sinners" the world over. To expect her intercession for a last-second, 50-yard "Hail Mary" touchdown reception is interesting in its irony, but seems pretty far-fetched when there are so many more important prayer- needs in our world. Nevertheless, our unbeliever brothers and sisters might wonder whether she has *any pull and with whom* to explain many of the events surrounding her life.

It is impossible to prove the existence of an afterlife for the non-believer. If it could be done, all of us would robotically fall into line and our freedom to believe or not would be snatched away. Nevertheless, the truly astounding occurrences associated with the life of Jesus on earth and his followers over the millenia, the inscrutable Shroud of Turino, and the unexplained cardiac muscle connected to Masses including one celebrated fourteen hundred years apart from the first speak loudly to those of us willing to listen. Moreover, the apparitions connected with Mary and miracles attributed to hundreds of martyrs and holy men and women over the centuries very compellingly argue for something beyond planet Earth.

There are so many of these unexplained occurrences that even hard-core atheists would have to be likened to the proverbial ostrich if they didn't find them *at least interesting*.

The Catholic Church has taught that there is a rich connection between human reason and faith. Catholicism professes that what we believe in faith and what reason discovers are not only compatible, but benefit each other. Faith should not be fearful of reason, but trust it since, according to Pope Francis "the light of reason and the light of faith both come from God' and cannot contradict each other," so that "whenever the sciences – rigorously focused on their specific field of inquiry – arrive at a conclusion which reason cannot refute, faith does not contradict it." The Church teaches that God is the source of both faith and reason, and there is no contradiction in God. Both faith and reason lead us to the one Truth who is God.

Scientific inquiry has based most research on a null hypothesis which assumes that there is no God as they seek the truth about the universe. The safer assumption set up for investigation should be that there *is* a God and atheist researchers are willing to keep an open mind in their studies and conclusions. The sheer wonders of the universe that they discover could lead them to ask along the way, "If you're out there, God, help my unbelief." Many of us believers are certain they will get the help they need.

Letter to Two of
My Non-Catholic Friends About My Catholic Faith

John F. Fisher, MD

October 27, 2007

Dear Andy and David,

I consider you both brothers in Our Lord Jesus Christ because you not only "talk the talk" but each of you "walks the walk" as well. You set a marvelous example for someone like me. I thank you for inviting me to the program given by a well-known Christian evangelist. I'm certainly interested in hearing a message which might speak to my own life's circumstances and motivate me to be more open to what God wants to do with me. I feel certain your speaker would provide me some previously uncharted avenues for prayerful reflection. I must decline your kind invitation, however, and I will now attempt to explain why I cannot feel fully comfortable in such a setting.

I am confident that the Good Lord completely understands where you both are in terms of your own personal relationships with Him. From what I know of you, you are both further along on your journey than I. He knows most likely better than you do, David, the set of circumstances which led you to separate yourself from the Catholic Church so many years ago. I feel certain, Andy, that He is pleased with the special man you have become and absolutely understands how you got there. If all of us, your friends, can see so readily that Jesus has top priority in your lives, I'm sure it is obvious to Him as well. Nevertheless, all three of us know that we have only scratched the surface of the life He intends us to live. You lads might be on second base. I feel like I'm heading down to first. But all of us are far from home compared to some of His followers who are alive on earth now or who have preceded us. I can name some of them and I bet you can too.

I do not fear that I might hear a message which would shake my Catholic faith by attending the worship service to which you both have so kindly invited me. However, whenever I hear a Christian message from a minister or other speaker who is not Catholic, I feel a sense of emptiness inside myself and a sadness for the speaker. The speaker might have the stature and the personal charisma and eloquence of Billy Graham, but for me the void remains. That emptiness stems from the fact that the message is missing something. For me that something is the absence or even rejection of a Eucharist- centered life. The sadness is that the speaker is missing a special relationship with Jesus he could otherwise have—the very personal one he frequently preaches to all of us about.

David, as a former Catholic, you will immediately understand the void I feel. Andy, you probably will not, although this subject has come up in our discussions in the past. So, I will address each of you separately in my explanation.

Dave: You were most likely taught about transubstantiation growing up and made your first communion by rote like I did and continued perfunctorily as I did through our early years. Apparently, you continued to do so through adulthood finally rejecting Catholicism altogether in the prime of your life. I don't see how you could ever have believed or fully understood the significance of that sacrament, Dave. If you once truly believed in the Real Presence of Jesus in the Eucharist, you couldn't possibly have left it and the Catholic Church behind. So, I will assume you never did believe and that you left the church, in part, for the reasons that you gave in your essay entitled, "Why I Changed My Dogtags." I will never forget the vitriol expressed in that writing, Dave, because it was so out of character for the gentle Christian you are. There was so much anger in what you wrote that I felt there was actually more to the story that you didn't write about. I wondered whether someone or some set of personal circumstances caused you to "get mad and leave the Church." You went so abruptly from very involved (ie Vice-president of our Catholic Physician's Guild with appearances on EWTN) to hatred of the Church. Notwithstanding those facts, when you were receiving Holy Communion, you must have only been going through the motions without genuine belief. You once belonged to a Church whose centerpiece of worship is mass and the Eucharist. It would be preposterous, laughable, and sacrilegious to worship in that way if transubstantiation does not occur. I believe it does and, as you well know, the Church has taught this since the First Century, but you must believe it does not. Without that belief, Dave, you cannot—you should not-- be a Catholic. While I shall always be rather puzzled and saddened by your break and the path you have followed since then, I hope you can understand the void I refer to when I hear evangelists speak whose "personal relationship with Jesus" does not include the Eucharist. If I'm correct in my belief, I can have *the most personal relationship with my Savior available on this earth* every day of my life at mass if I want to. Believe me, Dave, I want to and I am certain it has made all the difference in my life. I challenge you to find your own quiet time to pray to our Gentle Savior without any thought of the past in a humble and earnest way: "Lord, if you are truly present in the Eucharist and You want me to make personal contact with You by receiving You in this way, please let me know." Dave, if I'm correct, this is a prayer which will be answered in the affirmative before you depart this life.

Andy: I don't expect you to believe that Our Lord and Savior, Jesus Christ is actually present on the altar at a Catholic mass when the priest repeats the words of Jesus at the Last Supper, but faithful Catholics do believe this. We believe that Jesus as the triune God, the creator of the ingredients of bread and wine, through His minister, the priest, changes those elements into His very body and blood at each mass for us who participate in this liturgy. After that moment in the celebration, these simple elements remain bread and wine only in appearance; they actually become His very own body and blood. They have changed substance (ie transubstantiation). The closest analogy I can come up with, Andy, is a poor one, but take, for instance, a rectangular piece of cotton cloth. When the cotton fibers were woven together it became a simple piece of cloth. However, if you paint the Stars and Stripes on that cloth, it will never be a piece of cloth again. It has changed substance. It has forever become "Old Glory" -- our American Flag. When you receive Our Blessed Savior, Jesus Christ, in the Eucharist, you indeed have a 'Holy Communion' with Him and make genuine personal contact with your Savior of the most intimate kind. I like to think of it as His molecules becoming part of my own building blocks. I don't expect you to believe in transubstantiation, Andy, because it's a concept which has been drummed out of Protestant Christianity since the 1500s. So, for the last 500+ years good Protestant people have simply not raised their children to even think of it at all. Nowadays, transubstantiation isn't even a dim memory in Protestant households. A symbolic remnant of it shows up occasionally in Protestant services such as "the Lord's Supper" usually reverently celebrated once a month as a sincere prayerful symbol of what Jesus did at the Last Supper. Andy, that doesn't change the fact that the belief that Jesus Himself is truly present in the consecrated bread and wine has been around since the First Century. In about 56 AD—a little over 20 years after Jesus rose from the dead--, Paul (1Cor 11: 23-7) wrote probably the first description of what the Catholic Church has done for 2000 years every day: "For I received from the Lord what I also handed on to you, that the Lord Jesus, on the night he was handed over, took bread, and, after he had given thanks, broke it and said, 'This is my body that is for you. Do this in remembrance of me.' In the same way also the cup, after supper, saying, 'This cup is the new covenant in my blood. Do this, as often as you drink it, in remembrance of me.' For as often as you eat this bread and drink the cup, you proclaim the death of the Lord until he comes. Therefore, whoever eats the bread or drinks the cup of the Lord unworthily will have to answer for the body and blood of the Lord. A person should examine himself, and so eat the bread and drink the cup." For evidence that the early Church took the belief in transubstantiation literally, in 106 AD, Ignatius of Antioch (one of the early Church fathers who was taught by Polycarp, a disciple of John the Apostle) wrote in his *Epistle to the Smyrnians* (still in existence): "…They even abstain from the Eucharist and the public prayer (which later became known as the mass), because they will not admit that the Eucharist is the self-same body of our Savior Jesus Christ, which [flesh] suffered for our sins…" In ~ 155 AD, Justin Martyr, early Christian apologist, gave us the first written account of the liturgy (order of mass) when he wrote in his *First Apology*, p. 62 "…the food which is blessed by the prayer of His word, and from which our blood and flesh by transmutation are nourished, is the flesh and blood of that Jesus who was made flesh."

Andy, the belief in transubstantiation was universally held in the Church for its first 1500 years. Following the Reformation, the Eucharist disappears from Protestant worship. I ask you, *how does something revered as true and pivotal to worship for 1500 years suddenly become untrue with the Reformation?* Before the Reformation, Andy, Christians went to mass. The scripture was only available to the people during the prescribed readings at mass—Old and New Testament (It still is and there's actually more of Sacred Scripture at each mass than at most Protestant services today). The priest commented about those readings and their relevance and interpretation at mass. That's how they worshipped—like it orbelieve it or not! There were no bibles for people to carry around in the 1500s. Most of the Christian world couldn't even read until the 19th Century. Bible study groups like BSF are wonderful, but they areproducts of the modern world we live in. They are far from an age- old practice.

Virtually all Catholic scholars would agree that real problems and abuses existed in the Catholic Church at the time of Martin Luther and the others. Andy, did the Church need to be cleansed of the Eucharist? Was the Eucharist one of the abuses? I think that when the Reformers broke away in their well-intentioned effort to cleanse the Church, they inadvertently "threw the baby out with the bathwater. "Result—20,000. Protestant denominations, not one with a belief in transubstantiation; not one with the Eucharist as it has always been understood in the Catholic Church. You may not view that as tragic, but I do, Andy. I hope you now understand the void I feel when I hear non-Catholics talk about my Blessed Lord who I believe earnestly desires to give Himself to us in Holy Communion. I don't think you can worship Him any more completely than to hear His words of the Last Supper at mass and receive into yourself the "Lamb of God who takes away the sins of the world."

Just for a moment, Andy, whether you think such a miracle is preposterous or not, assume that it is true—even if you are just humoring me. If the Eucharist really is the Sacred Body and Blood of Our Savior and you have believed in it and received it all your life, how could you leave it? — ever. It would be like saying, "I don't care, Jesus, whether you left me this Eucharist or not. I don't care whether the Eucharist is Your special way for me to stay in close contact with You and have a real personal relationship with You all my life or not. I don't need it. I don't want it." If transubstantiation actually happens and Jesus is genuinely present and you believe it, you _have_ to be a Catholic, Andy. To do otherwise is essentially to "thumb your nose" at Jesus. If transubstantiation does not happen and Jesus is not actually present or you don't believe it, you _should not be_ a Catholic under any circumstances.

Andy, your sweet wife had the courage to become a Christian once upon a time. Do you have the courage to pray to Our Lord as I challenged Dave to pray above? I will pray that you do the next weekdays I am at 7:00AM mass at St. Mary's because I am convinced that the Eucharist will take you to a relationship with Jesus you never dreamed possible. Who knows? I may look around in the church and find you and Dave kneeling there with us someday soon.

On the outside chance that you have any interest in finding out more, I am enclosing a gift copy of a book entitled, _Rome Sweet Home_ written by Scott and Kimberly Hahn for each of you. Scott was a Presbyterian minister and bible scholar with his own congregation who hated the Catholic Church and determined to prove its teachings in error through the Scripture. He tried unsuccessfully to attack the teachings, one by one even with the help of his seminary professors. He decided that Catholicism was the truth and joined the Church. He now teaches Scripture at Franciscan University in Steubenville, OH, and is truly a renowned and extensively published Scripture scholar. Kimberly, after initial reluctance, joined her husband in the Catholic faith. *Rome Sweet Home* is an explanation of their journey to Catholicism. Ironically and apropos of this discussion, they are coming to St. Mary-on-the Hill Church, Saturday, January 26, 2008 to give a morning program. I will happily purchase tickets for the event for you and your wives if you will accept my invitation. I admit it's pretty unfair to invite you to our program and reject yours, but I do hope my explanation does help you understand my reasons. I can't help but believe that the Catholic Church continues to have the full repository of Christian doctrine and opportunities for His grace which Our Lord wanted for his followers and I need it all desperately. I also know He desired us all to be one and not 20,000 + denominations of Christianity (John 17: 11: "And now I am no more in the world, but these are in the world, and I come to thee. Holy Father, keep through thine own name those whom thou hast given me, that they may be one, as we [are].").

Thank you for your friendship over the years, Lads, and all the best—
Yours in Him, John

Fish Man: Random Perspectives from an Old-School Doctor—On Being a Doctor

John Fremont Fisher, MD

Medical College of Virginia Class of 1969 Virginia

Commonwealth University

Origins of the Compleat Physician: Caricature or Reality?

John F. Fisher MD

South Med J 2004; 97: 1165-8

Fellow faculty, parents, guests, and young colleagues: I am greatly honored to have been invited to be the guest speaker on the occasion of your initiation into our special fraternity. In case it crossed your mind, our president has very properly vetoed any semblance of hazing for admission to this fraternity, and you will not be asked as part of the ceremony to swallow a live crawdad as sophomores have been lobbying for, spend the night on a slab in the gross anatomy lab, or sing *Vesti la Giuba* in karaoke, which the faculty thought would be entertaining.

At this ceremony, which is about coats, I am reminded of the Irishman who went up to the clerk in the Men's Department at Macy's in New York City looking to find a bargain in a suit. He said, "Show me the cheapest suit in the store," and the fella said, "You're wearing it." And, brothers and sisters, in a little while, you, too, will be wearing something, and it may not be made of the finest and most expensive fabric—it may be made of ordinary and inexpensive cotton, but it is functional and easy to clean and it symbolizes something of great value. I like to think of it as a garment, which, when donned in the right spirit, changes the person who wears it forever. An analogy would be like that of a piece of cloth cut in a rectangle. It's just a piece of cloth. But when it is adorned with stars and stripes in red, white, and blue, it can never again be just a piece of cloth. Forevermore, it will be our national ensign—the American flag. Similarly, putting on the garment of a physician should be more than ceremony; it should change the very fiber of the young man or woman called to become a doctor. It is your decision, freely made, to take upon yourself the responsibility of the life and well-being of your fellow man. And, if this is not your motivation—if you are doing this to please your father or your mother—get out!

Many of you come from families rife with high achievers, and it has been expected from the childhood long lost in your subconscious that you, too, will become a successful professional. Your parents saw to it, often at great sacrifice to themselves, that you attended the finest schools in your area, and they demanded excellence from you. In some instances, those demands were rather subtly expressed, such as disappointment in your grade of A-minus instead of an A. In others, more overt pressure was applied, and there were severe consequences for mediocrity or bad grades. In the healthiest of circumstances, your parents told you that they would be satisfied with any grade you made if they knew you had done your best. It is almost instinctive in us parents to want our children to succeed, and the love we have for you is indescribable. When you look into the eyes of your own children one day, you will experience what we mean. You are extensions of our very selves, and you are our badges of self- worth. We can hardly help wanting you to shine above the rest because then we can shine above the rest, too. When you were kids, it might have been in music or dance or in baseball, football, soccer, swimming, golf, or tennis. Your every triumph somehow made us feel superior to other parents and gave some of us that certain confident air and condescending tone. When our eyes were not riveted on you, we might benevolently grant an audience to parents of kids who were not stars, dropping them a few bones of disingenuous encouragement, faint praise, and advice. A few of us have even been quite vicious in our competitiveness by anyone's standards, and, unintentionally, we may have passed that unfortunate trait on to you. In youth sports, you may have at first cringed when you heard us holler at the ref and then you learned to do it yourself. But it was all about you. As college got closer, we still cared about your sports and so on, but it was your grades in the high school AP courses and your score on the SAT that now mattered most. We were beside ourselves at your success in these areas, and we just couldn't stop talking about you to our friends. While pretending to listen intently as they talked about their children, we heard not a word and were just waiting for an opening to start in again about you. College sports focused and sharpened that competitive energy and in some, brought out downright hostility. But after the tumult and the shouting and the beer, it was back to the books to put your competitive nature to a more useful purpose. Now it was your GPA or your score on the MCAT that for us filled awkward silences and small talk at cocktail parties. No matter how hard we try, where you are concerned, we just can't "put a sock in it." Please forgive us if we have been a little too enthusiastic in our promotion of you. Whether our motives have been reasonable or questionable, all we ever wanted is for you to be a success.

And succeed you did. Your real friends were happy for your academic triumphs. Your fair-weather friends were happy for you too, especially if their grade was slightly higher than yours, but they would never ask. Your acquaintances, however, were full of "friendly" inquiries like, "How'd ya do?"or "What'd ya get?" Their one and only concern was that they scored higher than you. Gore Vidal was pretty insightful, (wasn't he?) when he said, "Every time a friend succeeds, I die a little." I'm reminded of the story about the two guys out in the middle of nowhere on a mountainous trail; they spot a hungry mountain lion running hard after them about a quarter of a mile off. After panicking at first and trying desperately to escape while the mountain lion is steadily gaining on them, one of them stops, sits down on a tree stump, and takes out a pair of running shoes from his backpack and puts them on. His buddy says, "What are you putting those shoes on for? You can't outrun that mountain lion!" The other guy says, "I know, but I don't have to outrun him. All I have to do is outrun you." And you all outran a lot of people to get to sit in that chair today. And you just got here, and you're thinking that now you really need to turn it on because you need to outrun about 180 more to land that premier residency you may want three or four years from now. And after you get to Yale or the Mass General or to Stanford for your

postgraduate training, you'll be the best, won't you? And think of the conversational mileage we parents will get out of your accomplishments at other cocktail parties or in that two-page family update we send to all our relatives and people we barely know along with our holiday greeting cards. And as for you, you will have been trained by some clinicians and scientists who have written 500 or more scientific articles and who have 20 or 30 groupies hanging on them at all the big meetings laughing at all their jokes and hoping for a sentence or even a glance directed their way. They'll teach you and inspire you to be just like them because that's what academic medicine is all about. Isn't it? Admiration? Praise? Recognition? Or if a career in a teaching institution isn't your cup of tea, you'll certainly feel you are more than prepared to enter private practice, and, with your hard-fought credentials, how can you miss being part of the best group practice in any city you choose? You should be able to write your own ticket and be able to pay back all those loans quickly and get your wife or husband out of the rat race they've been in putting you through all your training. With your competitive edge over the rest of them and hard-work ethic, you ought to easily be able get that house with the pool, pay the
$35,000 initiation fee at the country club, get that silver Jag you've always wanted, and put a large down payment on your house at the beach or in the mountains. Furthermore, you'll have your children perfectly timed and ready for you to live vicariously in them just like we did in you.

Have you noticed what the missing element in all this competitive success I've just described is? Yes, it's the patient. It is the patient who has been left in your wake as you jet ski by. In the academic medical center there really are some of us physicians (hopefully very few) who use medical knowledge about patients more to publish in esteemed periodicals primarily for self-aggrandizement. Most of the physicians in an academic medical center, whether faculty or house staff, are salaried. If one is salaried, it is only human nature to desire to be well paid while not having to work too hard. Such an attitude is common and usually pretty benign. However, this particular attitudinal tumor can become quite malignant and life-threatening. It can be diagnosed in one's self easily. Later in your career, if you actually find yourself feeling that you don't want to see a patient for any reason at any time unless you absolutely have to, you have the full-blown cancer. In other physicians, the symptoms and signs are less obvious. They may be short with you or with the nurses over the phone or critical of the care given to the patients by you or other physicians. They commonly want to transfer patients to other physicians. Translation: They really don't want to be bothered. Expect the tumor to metastasize around the medical school hospital if doctors with a true calling to help sick people are few in number, inundated with more patients than they can carefully evaluate, or not in key supervisory positions. If those other brand of physicians and trainees become plentiful or gain a good foothold, medical emergencies, hospital admissions, or calls in the middle of the night become viewed as negative interruptions. A good day on- call to these physicians is Mexican food delivered to the hospital and getting to watch television while the beeper and phone remain silent. An opposite but equally malignant state can occur in the private practice setting. Motivated by big mortgages on ostentatious houses and driven by a desire for fine clothing, fancy cars, and exotic vacations, some community physicians, again hopefully very few, are rationalizing and justifying expensive procedures on patients for very marginal indications—on insured patients, that is. Indigent patients without a pay source must have unequivocal evidence that a procedure is required and even then are tended to when the doctor gets time. Better still, that patient is transferred to the medical school hospital as "too complex to handle" in the community hospital. Other doctors without an expensive procedure they can charge for are seeing patients in an assembly-line fashion, running them through the turnstiles at warp speed, looking at their watches while their sick or depressed brothers and sisters are trying to explain what's troubling them, doing cursory examinations, and then sending them out with a preprinted prescription for an antibiotic, a stomach acid blocker, a cholesterol-lowering agent, and an antidepressant. Don't these patients understand? I've got a tee time at 12:45! And, by the way, payment is expected at the time of service and Medicaid has become so complicated that it can no longer be accepted.

These are obviously gross exaggerations and I can only speak with experience about the Medical College of Virginia and the University of Cincinnati where I trained, the military and community hospitals where I have worked, and my beloved Medical College of Georgia, where I have spent most of my 38 years in medicine. At each of these institutions and especially in ours here in Augusta, I have found vastly more of the genuinely dedicated men and women, young and old, with a true vocation to take care of the hurting, the sick, and the dying, than I have that occasional self-centered individual who may possess an MD degree but who will likely never become a doctor. I engage in negative hyperbole only to emphasize something in which I firmly believe: Medicine should be our own unique way of loving and serving the people with whom we share this planet. For some of us in this room, it will also be our way of serving God. The same can and should be said of all honest work. But in our profession, like none other, our fellow human beings may entrust us with intimate and personal details about themselves that they might share with no one else. They permit us to perform sometimes uncomfortable and embarrassing examinations or bravely submit to excruciatingly painful operations just so that we might find a way to help them. Rarely do they check our credentials because they believe in us, many with the faith of children. And that, my dear young colleagues, is a sacred trust for which we must be prepared. My challenge for you today is to rethink all this. Just for a moment, see if you can feel the sleeves of that white jacket when you put it on as it clings to your arms or the collar as it touches the back of your neck. Let it be the symbol of a new you—a young doctor, a doctor-in-training to be sure, but a young doctor nonetheless— certainly not something called a "health care provider." Let the donning of that coat be an epiphany for you, starting now. For the rest of your life, promise yourself to learn about the human body, but to learn for a purpose that is pure and good and true. Remain in awe about the body's complexity, with every human cell a universe in itself. Allow your sense of awe to strengthen your faith if you have one or to at least make you wonder if you have none. Study not because someone's admiration may depend on what you know, but because someone's life may depend on it. You already have many virtues. Be sure that humility is one of the virtues that you are especially known for. Recognize that your bright mind is not your own doing, but it is something that has been given to you. Even with all your intelligence, have the humility to admit that you cannot know it all. Use that humility to ask that "dumb question," but maybe dramatically enhance your understanding of something important. Use it to say, "I don't know" when you don't and then have the curiosity to follow the "I don't know" with "I'll find out." Have the humility to realize that you need the help of all of us who wear the white coat and we need you in return. Humility is not about being full of yourself; it's about emptying yourself for others. Those physicians from the tuberculosis hospitals of the 19th century knew full well that they could likely die themselves of TB; for they knew it was contagious and had no cure, but, heroically, they kept tending to the sick anyway. So have all those brave doctors on countless battlefields and on-board ships in wartime. They emptied themselves. "Greater love than this no man hath; that he lay down his life for his friend." The knowledge of each of us in this room (though in some of us it is dissipating fast) casts a shadow, but our shadows don't precisely overlap. Each of us has something to share. I implore you to share your knowledge by helping your classmates understand something you do—and rooting for them all. Humility is making Gore Vidal eat his words by changing them into "every time a friend succeeds, so do I." I've asked you to think about that white coat changing you. Now think for a moment what it means when your sick or hurting patient sees you in it. It changes him; for when you walk in the room in that coat, whether you deserve it or not, he sees a person with wisdom and vast knowledge, with compassion and hope and relief from his suffering and from his fear of the unknown. It's quite a pedestal he has placed you on before you even introduce yourself. That is the legacy that the great physicians who have worn a white coat before you have led him to believe. It's as if they've put that coat on you themselves. You cannot let your patient down. You cannot let those wonderful physicians in our fraternity who came before you down. You've got to live up to those great expectations. Start with a friendly handshake and a kind word or two and then just listen. There's an old adage that remains sage diagnostic advice today, "Listen to the patient; he is telling you the diagnosis." You can't listen if your mind is already made up or if you're looking at the clock or if you are constantly in a rush. Then, examine your brother or sister with care and with sensitivity. Be sure you know what's normal and when you are not sure, don't gloss over it and call it normal like so many of us do. Get your physical diagnosis book out and look it up or ask for help. Read about your patient's symptoms and findings if you need to and enjoy the challenge of figuring out exactly what's wrong—kind of like Lieutenant Columbo. Once you've got the problem solved, choose the best treatment for your special patient. If you're not sure what you are treating, stop treating it! Get some help.

And if you seem to always be in a rush, ask yourself why and fix it. There are those outside our hallowed halls, our hospital wards, and our examination rooms who look at medicine today as a business that can be made more profitable to themselves and their shareholders by slashing overhead and giving us android voices who answer the telephone and drag us and our patients through a maze of endless menus with minimal hope of talking to a human, let alone a doctor or a nurse. These tycoons or the federal "G-Men" want us seeing as many patients who can pay as rapidly as possible and seeing a minimum of patients who can't pay. They expect us to justify in writing because we have prescribed certain expensive medications. They are skeptical about certain imaging studies we order and will not pay for a day in the hospital beyond what their black book says is the statistical average length of stay for a given diagnosis. If we are willing to hack our way through the thicket of their company's telephone version of "Where's Waldo" or visit their web site, that is, if we can remember our user ID and password (they are "kind enough" to e-mail our password back to us soon, if we've forgotten it) or fill out a confusing array of forms written in double-speak, they might condescend to permit us to care for patients as we see fit. They are very poor stewards of our time. I wonder—could it be on purpose? Are they simply trying to wear us down? These business executives only think they know medicine, and they see us in the white coats, not as allies, but as adversaries—as part of the liabilities of their ideal profit centers. In reality, some of them are lay people practicing medicine without a license on patients they've never seen. Ironically, when the tables are turned, and they or their loved ones are sick or hurting, they expect of us the most detailed histories, the most careful examinations, and the latest and best laboratory studies and x-rays that money can buy. Don Quixote de la Mancha was trying to joust with windmills that he imagined were monsters to save his beloved Dulcinea. In this case, our beloved profession is under assault by very real monsters, and those of us who understand what the white coat is all about must keep tilting at them whenever we get the chance.

I will leave you with an open letter to patients. Something like this, only maybe your own version, should be on proud display in your office one day:

My Dear Patients:

Thank you for the privilege of allowing me to participate in your care. I am deeply concerned for your well-being and want to relieve your suffering if I am able. To do that, I will try my best to ascertain the cause of your trouble. If the cause is not immediately obvious, I will ask you to carefully describe your discomfort until I am certain I understand what you mean. I may need to ask many other questions about you and your family to try to determine what might be wrong. For minor problems, I may do only a limited examination. If I believe you do not truly need prescription medications, I will not prescribe them, especially when I am uncertain what is wrong. Only if I believe prescription medications will hasten your recovery or relieve your symptoms, will I prescribe them. If I suspect a serious problem, I will do a detailed examination and spend whatever time with you that you need until it is safe to turn my attention elsewhere. Those of you who are waiting to see me, will simply have to wait, but most of you will understand that I would do the same for you. I can only hope that those who pay me for my time will also understand, but you, my brothers and sisters, come first. And if you become seriously ill, I will endeavor to be as certain about the cause as I am able, so that I may limit the medications to only those you truly need. When I am uncertain of your diagnosis, I will get help from colleagues who share my philosophy. If I cannot cure your disease, I will try my best to ease your suffering and to do you no harm. I believe that somehow our interaction was intended by God, sometimes for the positive influence I may have on you, but often for the positive influence you may have on me. For this reason, I am willing to participate in your care regardless of whether you share my views and regardless of how you got sick, your social standing, your race, your religious beliefs, or your ability to pay me or my employer. I am honored that you have chosen me to try to help you and I will try to be worthy of that confidence.

Sincerely,

Your devoted doctor of the Class of 2007

Medical School Graduates of 2006:
"Hooded, but not Hoodwinked"

John F. Fisher MD

South Med J 2006; 99: 909-10

During medieval times, the hood was used by all classes of people as a head covering with a shoulder cape to protect from the cold. It was eventually adopted by monks and university students and by the 15th century, had become a token of graduation. The word "wink" originally meant to close one's eyes. To be hoodwinked was to have one's eyes covered by one's hood. Thieves would "hoodwink" their victims to rob them. Now we all understand it to mean, "to deceive by false appearance." You will be hooded today, but whether or not you will be hoodwinked by your new profession or by life itself depends on you, for there are strong forces in our world which may distract you from the noble life of service you have chosen as a physician. My plea to you today is, "Don't let them." Recognize and defeat them before they can hoodwink you. All too soon it will be time to get down to the serious business of your life's work—being a doctor One of your most important choices will be choosing how you deal with your patients as you begin your career as a physician. What tone will you set? Patients come in all sizes, shapes, colors and smells, and with all varieties of personalities and personality disorders. But some patients may make you seriously question your choice of a vocation: for example, the 54-year-old, morbidly obese, depressed woman who seems to actually enjoy poor health with her endless litany of complaints. Perhaps because of the way you took care of her, she'll soon be seeking treatment at the institution where you matched. She liked you as her doctor so much that she'll magnify whatever complaint matches your specialty and your on-call schedule, be it Medicine, Dermatology,

Surgery, or Orthopaedics. Or perhaps not. Perhaps she sensed that you, like most of the doctors she's seen this year, didn't care for her or could feel your impatience with her as you tried to hurry her through her history. And what about the disheveled, belligerent drunk with rotten teeth, fetid breath, and cirrhosis who has ruined his life whom you will be called to see at 4:00 AM? When you enter his room, you will have a choice. Will you be his doctor? —or just a "healthcare provider" tired and irritated by him, by the hour, and by the fact that you are on- call and you have already gotten five "hits" that day. How will you describe your patient to your fellow interns before morning report? Will you say your night was horrible and call him a troll, a dump from another hospital, a train wreck, or some other subhuman term? I hope not because here is an opportunity to reveal the goodness which led you to medicine in the first place—that brought you to where you sit now. However unlikely, your unexpected kindness and compassion at that hour of the morning might just turn his life around. On the other hand, your lack of these virtues could just harden him further. You have chosen a profession which has called you to reach out in genuine love and respect for others. Your profession will call upon you to try to relieve suffering regardless of the potential danger to yourself, regardless of whether, in your opinion, your patients brought their illness on themselves, regardless of the hour, regardless of their beliefs or their color, and especially regardless of whether they can pay you. You have a choice with patients: Will you be a force for good or just a force to be reckoned with? Your patients are not the only ones who may test your mettle. You will inevitably encounter fellow interns who leave you with a lot of work as they check out to you; a few callous, hypercritical residents whom you can never seem to please, and overworked attendings who just want to get rounds over with and are not interested in hearing you present. How will you choose to react to the ward clerks, nurses, laboratory personnel, cafeteria workers, and department secretaries, all of whom have their own problems and may occasionally be less than considerate in their dealings with you? Someone in this group is bound to rub you the wrong way unless you are like St. Francis of Assisi, Mahatma Gandhi, Billy Graham, or Albert Schweitzer. The fire of that goodness is not just in those of us who take care of patients; it burns inside us all. It is manifested in many different ways: working hard and taking pride in our work, not caring who gets the credit; being generous with our time; being modest and not showy; giving anonymously; desiring the well-being, success, and prosperity of others; recognizing the importance of seemingly unimportant jobs held by others in our sphere; supervising others with truthfulness, patience, and good humor.

We all recognize that goodness. When others show it to us unexpectedly, we are touched and impressed by it. And we remember it. It is contagious and we often spread it to others and find that it brings out the best in them. Furthermore, in our humanness, we are likely to broadcast the good things we have done because it makes us feel good about ourselves. On the other hand, we can also be weak, arrogant, cruel, prejudiced, lazy, and unfeeling. Unfortunately, these traits are also contagious, but we don't want others to see them because we instinctively know they are not right. Why else would we try to hide our dark side? The goodness in us wants out. The shame of evil stays within.

Some of us are very certain how that goodness got there; others not so sure. It would be wise to ponder that crucial question either way. But, regardless of how our intrinsic goodness got there, it remains an indelible part of the human life force. Some of us cover it up; but none of us can escape it. People who would lead you away from your goodness are often attractive, laugh at all your jokes, and shower you with all sorts of false flattery, but they are wolves in sheep's clothing—they are your mortal enemies. Do not let them hoodwink you. The real joy in life does not come from a house at the beach or in the mountains, fine clothes, fine automobiles, fine country clubs, and valuable art work and possessions. It doesn't come from personal achievements or besting others. It comes from emptying ourselves of the goodness within and pouring it out on those with whom we share this planet. Why put off beginning to experience that real joy even one minute longer? If medicine has lost some of its luster in the last 20 years, it is because we physicians are not the role models we once were. So be a role model. Let the light shine from your heart and out your eyes. You will notice a change in the people around you: your patients, your fellow house officers, the medical students you will be responsible to teach, your attendings, the nurses, the ward clerks, and even the housekeeping staff. But equally important, you will notice a great change in yourself. Once this philosophy has become part of you, you will no longer be doing good for selfish reasons, but simply because it is the right thing to do.

I leave you with some words which paraphrase what Ralph Waldo Emerson wrote long ago as he endeavored to define success: It is to laugh often and much, to win the respect of intelligent people and the affection of children, to earn the appreciation of honest critics and endure the betrayal of false friends, to appreciate beauty, to find the best in others, to leave the world a bit better, whether by a healthy child, a garden patch, or a redeemed social condition; to know even one life has breathed easier because you have lived. This is to have succeeded!

May God bless each and every one of you and may your coffins be built of 100-year-old oaks which I will plant tomorrow.

A Doctor's Prescription

John F. Fisher MD

***Notre Dame Magazine*, Autumn 2022**

Three months or so after you finish your premedical studies and graduate, you will be seated in a large auditorium on the campus of the medical school you selected, and you'll once again be a freshman awaiting orientation. The school will have taken a flier on you, after reviewing your grades, accomplishments and extra-curriculars and reading your personal statement, because you fit their notion of the type of physician they want to produce. There you will launch the final leg of your journey, just four years away from fulfilling your dream. Some may wonder whether this dream might be a nightmare about to come true. So, stop for a moment. Pick up a pen. On a blank sheet of paper, slowly and painstakingly write your signature. Now add the letters M.D. or D.O. after it, and stare at it. While you are staring, think what this means to you, your family and, most of all, the many patients who will come under your care.

You haven't yet worked up (as we in the profession say) a single patient. I've been a physician since before you were born. I wonder what workup I'm on by now-my 400,000th? I also wonder if I haven't made at least some difference in the grand scheme of things. I hope so. For that's what this dream of medicine is all about, making a difference in the lives of our brothers and sisters on this planet. Medicine affords us the opportunity, like no other profession, to do just that-- to get to know people in the most personal and intimate way and make them better off for having known you. I hope you take that signature just as seriously when you're done with medical school as you do now.

You probably applied to several schools, and some asked why you want to be a doctor. You might have hesitated to say that you "want to help people," thinking that those who read your application would think your reason naieve, hokey, or unimaginative. But it's what you should have meant, whatever the half-truth you wrote in your essay. And it goes deeper than that. Medicine should be an expression of a genuine love of your fellow person - a real willingness to relieve someone else's suffering regardless of the danger that the effort might pose to you. Regardless also of how the suffering person got sick; of whether, in your opinion, she brought the illness on herself; of the hour or whether or not you were on call; of the patient's beliefs or anything else about her; and *especially* of whether she can pay you. I am reminded of the brave physicians who cared for tuberculosis patients with tenderness and compassion more than a century ago, knowing full well that they would likely get TB at some point themselves. "Greater love than this no man hath, that he lay down his life for his friends."

Anyone can want to help people who are trusting, cooperative and agreeable. Who doesn't want to take care of great patients who are stoic, who share your philosophy of life, who are attractive, who are celebrities of one sort or another or are members of the Augusta National? But what about the disheveled, belligerent drunk with rotten teeth and fetid breath who has ruined his life and whom you are called to see at 4 a.m. because he is sick? This is the sort of patient who separates the real doctors from the mere "health care providers." How will you speak to your colleagues about *him?* Will you call him a troll or a gomer or a dump from another hospital or a train wreck or whatever disparaging term might be in vogue when you hit the medical wards? I hope not, because here is an opportunity to show what you're made of, born of the conviction that I hope brought you to where you sit now: genuine love and respect for your fellow man. However unlikely it might be, your kindness and compassion might just turn this man's life around-and your lack of it could harden him further.

The bottom line is this: If you do not have genuine love in your heart for people, get out now. If you are in it for prestige or for a certain lifestyle or because your mother or father was a doctor, you may be brilliant and skilled and have all the tools, but medicine is not your true vocation. Go do something else.

For those of you who believe being a physician is your destiny, don't let medicine devour you. Don't take on more patients or responsibilities simply to make your car payments, mortgage payments or country club dues. You may hurt someone when you are overwrought. Instead, take good care of the number of patients you can handle and be content with the income that brings you. You won't starve. Your family will need you at home. Your children will need to be able to recognize you on sight.

Finally, don't allow yourself, like so many students, to suffer through med school, to be mean-spirited and cutthroat-competitive, to hope others did worse on an exam than you did, to whine, complain and count the days until you are through.

When you do hit the wards, don't be sucked in by an intern or resident who is angry at the world and considers a good night on call one when no patients need admission and who talks about patients as "hits"- as in, "How many hits did you get last night?" Some love of your fellow person *that* is.

You and I may not even be here tomorrow. If today is our last day on Earth, let's make it a day we can be proud of, when we live with a joyful outlook, give our responsibilities our best effort, and make the people who play a part in our life better off for having encountered us. And those people might be your patients, or they might be classmates, or your professors, or even the people who sweep up. Tomorrow will take care of itself. It's not easy to live this way, but you know I am speaking the truth. And if you embrace this philosophy, you will not find yourself wishing your life away as so many people do. You'll close your eyes each night less anxious about some far-off goal and really enjoy all the great people, moments and beauty on your life's journey. And one of these days, the Good Lord willing, you will sign your name with an M.D. or D.O. after it and really know what that means.

Final Destination: Life as a Physician.

Four Important Stops Along the Way

John F. Fisher MD

Address given to graduating class of 2021, Medical College of Georgia, Augusta University, May 13, 2021

President Keel, Dean Hess, Faculty Colleagues, Family and Friends of the Class of 2021: I am truly amazed and honored to have been chosen to speak to our young graduates on this great occasion.

This is your moment, Lads and Lasses—this is one of those important moments you have worked so hard for-- right now. Tomorrow your Mom or Dad will introduce you to people as, "This is my daughter, Dr. Shepp, Dr. Talkad, or this is my son, Dr. Butler or Dr. Wehrle. It'll be a proud month for your family during this 'honeymoon period.' When their friends ask your parents how they're doing, they will ever so subtly and matter-of-factly tell them they've just been to their son or daughter's medical school graduation. Please forgive them—they can't help it! I never could stop my own Mom from introducing me as, "This is my son, Dr. Fisher."

I would imagine that my path to Medicine was a lot different from yours. Thanks to my Irish Catholic mother, my early education was from the good sisters (I had mostly nuns for 12 years). For the first eight of those, I tried to keep on their good side because they were strict, bigger than I was, and took no prisoners for bad behavior.

I can see one instance 'Oh so clearly now'-- we'll call her Sister Mary Inquisition, my 8th grade teacher, how she stormed down the aisle after one notorious smart aleck who in religion class was talking and laughing devilishly during the reading of a biblical passage in which the word 'bosom' was mentioned. All I can say is that she physically wore him out!

But I thank most of those women in those medieval garments who were not cruel and had taken a vow of poverty working for 50 dollars a month plus room and board. They dedicated themselves to the Good Lord and to teaching young people and demanding excellence from us.

It was more of the same at St. Patrick High School except for one incident indelibly planted in my memory. During an English exam as a sophomore, Sister Melanie caught me with a piece of paper with answers on it passed across the aisle to me by a classmate. I didn't even get time to read it before she stormed down aisle and tore my exam paper in half and gave me an 'F.' I never did that again.

That same year our class was scheduled for elections to join the various city administrators like the mayor, city attorney, police chief, and city physician and shadow their activities for a day. I ran for City Physician mainly because my Uncle Bob, whom I admired, was a pediatrician and for no other good reason, but I won. Shadowing that doctor was pretty interesting. So after that, all my classmates assumed I wanted to be a doctor. I couldn't let them down. Nevertheless, the nuns had me ready for Notre Dame and pre-med.

At Notre Dame I got a dose of reality—three pink slips at mid- term of my first semester

I either had to study harder or study better. Singing in the Glee Club and traveling all over the country helped me _keep being me _and studying better.

Like they say in baseball, it was a close play at home, but the Big Umpire called me 'safe at home' and I got into medical school at the Medical College of Virginia in Richmond.

You might remember when we first met, I had you painstakingly write out your signature and put an MD behind it. I used to daydream about it and practice my signature over and over when I was a student. That's why I introduced it to you for your own daydreams four years ago. Well tomorrow, you can finally do that and mean it—exciting isn't it? But next month, after the honeymoon's over, you will begin to make a real contribution as a full-fledged doctor—your own personal contribution to your fellow person. You will promise to make that contribution in the oath that you will take shortly.

That's what your job is! Will you really mean what you say in that oath or will it be just a formality for the occasion?

Your training will not only be about getting the next job. It's about contributing something which is uniquely you to the sick, the suffering, or even the worried well. If *they* are your focus, you will automatically impress people, especially your students who will see you daily on their rotations. You can inspire them to be just like you. You can also turn them completely off! How they turn out is partly your responsibility. How seriously will you take that responsibility? And as for the next job, it'll come looking for *you!* And you'll likely land right where the Good Lord wants you to land. Even more amazingly--somehow you did the choosing. It happened to me in 1977 and I'm still around. I can't explain how that works, can you?

I've got four things I'd like to talk about with you today:

1. Digging Deep

2. Going to the Mat

3. Staying Curious

4. Making Time for Family and Yourself

Digging Deep

You have to dig deep inside yourself to take on all that's required of a doctor. Being on-call and in clinics and ERs can be crazy and it's easy to get behind—I was on-call every other night for 8 of the 12 months of my internship. A few of the attendings actually believed that the only thing wrong with every other night call was that you missed half the workups—yeah right!

Lots of interruptions. You get weary (mentally & physically).

One night I was trying to dig deep. I hadn't gone to bed and the ER called me for my 13th admission and 2nd with DKA. I found an empty room and just cried from stress and weariness. The kind head nurse, Ms. Pauline Hymenn, found me in there, gave me a pat on the back, and told me it would be all right. And she was right-- it was. After all, compared to some people in this world, _your_ yoke _is actually easy_ and _your burden is light_.

Going to the Mat

Go to the mat for your patients— but especially for the ones who give you a hard time. Anyone can work hard for attractive people who share your philosophy or for people who are wealthy and influential, or for celebrities of one sort or another. It would be only natural to try to impress them with the care you give them, not neglecting the smallest detail in examining them, explaining what you think might be their problem at great length, following up on their progress as promised, contacting them by phone, and trying to stay connected to them forever. Let's face it, if somebody important were your patient, or even better, became _your friend_, you would relish in it—admit it!

But what about the hostile, intoxicated man with a cough, bad teeth, and fetid breath? The homeless iv drug addict with a fever? The abusive parent with a screaming baby? How will you deal with them? Will you go to the mat for them? Don't they really deserve the same level of care that you gave to the member of the Augusta National? Just saying!

Wherever you are headed next month, each of you has it in you to become "Chief Resident" by going to the mat for each of your patients without whining and complaining.

How do you think these young physicians rose to the top and got that designation? But even if no one seems to recognize that you always go to the mat for your patients, God does. Not a bad audience that!

Staying Curious

Stay curious. Have the attitude of Sherlock Holmes and you will avoid burnout because you're constantly trying to solve clinical puzzles, some of them quite fascinating.

Remember--70% of diagnoses are made from history. Don't stop inquiring about the patient's chief complaint until you understand it better than the patient does. That's the key to which system went afoul. You don't have time to do a "world-class" physical on every system of the body in every patient. You do have time to do a "world-class" physical on the system which went afoul. I think it's malpractice if you don't.

Don't miss the carotid bruit in an elderly lady who's dizzy. Be determined to find that palpable spleen in a teenager with a sore throat. If you don't find it, maybe that spleen will rupture in a contact sport. It'd be hard to forgive yourself for missing that. When you abbreviate within normal limits with 'WNL,' don't let it mean, "We never looked." If the problem is cough and shortness of breath in a person brought in after a motor vehicle accident, don't miss the hollow, tympanitic percussion note of a pneumothorax—especially a tension pneumothorax. If they die, you may never get over it.

Don't avoid that rectal or pelvic exam in a person with abdominal pain just because it's embarrassing or awkward. It may give you the answer as to the cause.

And have some fun with your chosen profession. See if you can predict what the chest x-ray, EKG, or labs will show after you've taken a history and examined the patient. Have some fun with your students by making them do the same.

Be aggressive and gentle at the same time with your physical exam skills. Look hard for something the patient with that history should have—that retinal lesion in a person who's vision has become blurry, that S3 gallop in someone who's short of breath, that axillary node in a woman with a lump in her breast. Find that faint murmur in a patient with a fever of unknown origin. Find that abdominal bruit and the pulsatile mass in an old man with back pain and thready pulses.

Have the attitude of a doctor on a mission. For example, in an old man with iron deficiency, approach the patient with this attitude: "If you've got a cancer in your colon, Mr. Smith, I'm gonna find that mass in your abdomen. With that kind of attitude, not much gets by you. It's so satisfying and invigorating when you make even little discoveries—protects you against burnout.

Make some time looking at the microscopy of body fluids—especially in a really sick patient when time is of the essence. The lab has only a few minutes to process a Gram stain because they have so many. Take it from me--they do occasionally miss stuff. Look at the blood film of your anemic patients yourself. Look at the blood film of a returned traveler with fever yourself--You don't want the lab to call you up and tell you your patient has malaria. You'd feel so much better if you looked at the smear, found it yourself, and the lab confirmed it.

So, take ownership of each of your patients—After all, the buck should stop with you. If _you_ won't do it, someone else will take over and, down deep, you won't feel very good about it.

Don't be only a computer report type of physician—reading some report and looking up the treatment on *Up-to-Date*. That's not fascinating. Doctors like that are headed for burnout.

When time permits, go to Radiology or MRI and go over the images with the radiologists. Go to Pathology and have the pathologist show you why your patient has cancer. Go over your leukemia patient's bone marrow with the hematologist. These are professors—make them profess!

Stay curious and you'll be amazed at what you can find and what you can learn.

Keep track of some fascinating patient cases. Write them up when you have time. You can *do this*, Dr. Sherlock!!!

Make Time for Family and Yourself

Minimize day care as much as you can. No one can love your kids the way you do. They *are you* in so many ways! They'll repay that love a hundredfold. They might even want to live and raise their kids where you live because they love being around you and want to always be part of your life. Take it from me—you just turn around and they're grown and gone from you.

Have dinner together as often as possible. Go to their performances and school events. Go to their games. They'll know you're there even without you yelling at the ref or the umpire. Read to them often whether it's Dr. Seuss, Beatrix Potter, The Giving Tree, The Chronicles of Narnia, Grimm's Fairy Tales, or Treasure Island. It's OK for them to fall asleep. It's OK for you to get sleepy along with them. They'll never forget you used to do this with them.

Keep being you by doing the activities you have always loved whether it's biking or hiking, gardening, painting, hunting, fishing, dancing, playing golf, playing tennis, playing music, going to concerts, or even singing. This is an essential antidote for physician burnout.

"Oh! One more thing."

I challenge each one of you to become "Intern of the Year" wherever you go to train. You most likely, at least, will be one of the finalists with this attitude: *Nobody* can take better care of your patients than you do. *Nobody* recognizes the help of your nurses and nursing assistants more often than you do. *Nobody* acknowledges the help of ward clerks, lab techs, or even environmental services staff as frequently as you do. Remember--We're all in this thing together!

I have truly found that the rewards of taking care of patients and their families and teaching young people about them are too numerous to count-- and so will you.

Allowing me to share some of my own thoughts and experiences with you on this great day has been very special for an old geezer like me and I thank you. God Bless, Lads and Lasses.

On Medical Education

The Medical Ethics of Poor Supervision

John F. Fisher, MD

South Med J 2020; 113:372-3

Medical trainees expect to become competent physicians like their professors, most of whom facilitate those goals. A rare, unscrupulous supervisor can eschew the bedside and practice medicine largely from a keyboard. Carefully worded notes pasted into the electronic medical record can disguise this charade. Pedantic mini- lectures outside patient rooms can impress young learners and further divert attention from the patient who may suffer in this hands-off approach. Consequently, compassion for sick people, the art of history taking, and the subtleties of physical examination may never be demonstrated to eager student doctors.

Hypothetical Scenario

Sam Gavonovich's second day on Medicine was his first ever as a clinical clerk. Orientation made him miss attending rounds yesterday. With not a little foreboding, he was to present Mr. O'Reilly today. He had presented standardized patients with scripted, faux problems to Physical Diagnosis preceptors, but Mr. O'Reilly was the real deal and his attending was the notorious Dr. Hansen. The team stared expectantly at Sam outside O'Reilly's room at 11:45 AM. Dr. Hansen, glancing at his watch, said, "Who has Mr. O'Reilly?" Tremulously, Sam uttered a barely audible, "Mr. O'Reilly is a 49-year-old male admitted yesterday for severe abdominal pain. "Male what?" interjected Dr Hansen, "Man is the correct term!" Flustered, Sam continued. "The pain is mid-abdominal. He endorses nausea and anorexia, but fails to endorse fever, night sweats, cough, or painful urination." "What do you mean endorses, Mr. Gavonovich?" Does he approve of his nausea and anorexia?" "No, sir," he said timidly. In the palpable silence, Sam gathered himself and went on. "His history reveals a VA admission for abdominal pain. He takes no medications, has no allergies, and drinks socially. "His review of 'symptoms' is positive for stuffy nose and a toothache on the right and negative for chest pain, rashes, suicidal thoughts, and edema." "Systems, not symptoms!"

exclaimed Hansen. Sam continued, "On physical exam, his vital signs were stable, chest was clear; heart was regular rate and rhythm. His bowel sounds were present, but, because he was writhing in pain, I couldn't localize it and I'm not sure about hepatomegaly. His joints were intact and his neurological was non-focal."

"And what's your diagnosis?" Dr. Hansen queried condescendingly. "I'm favoring appendicitis, sir," said Sam. Accustomed to dishing out public humiliation, Dr. Hansen scoffed, "Baloney! This patient needs a doctor!"

With Sam's face flushed and heart pounding, the team entered the room, and Dr. Hansen, looking again at his watch, asked Mr. O'Reilly about his belly pain, only half-listening. He prodded several areas of the abdomen, agreed with the resident's impression of acute pancreatitis and its treatment. Avoiding eye contact with Sam or anyone on the team, he typed on the nearest computer: "History reviewed; patient examined. No fever, chills, or sweats; no diarrhea, constipation, or hematochezia; no cough, chest pain, or dyspnea. Agree with assessment and plans as outlined by house staff." He billed the patient at CPT (Current Procedural Terminology) code 99233 and headed for noon conference. The team disbursed, learning nothing except to wear full metal jackets on future rounds with Hansen. Fellow third-year, Mary Kate Green, patted Sam's shoulder sympathetically, and Sam, crestfallen, walked across the street to McDonald's, nowhere near noon conference.

Discussion

This depiction of modern attending rounds is obvious hyperbole. Mr. O'Reilly is the ultimate victim because Sam did not know how to take a proper history and his attending was too busy billing. A careful history should yield at least 70% of diagnoses[1], but not the kind of history Sam and Hansen took. Sam may have deflected some of Hansen's pejorative flack if a Physical Diagnosis preceptor had insisted on a consistent rigor on his oral presentations and write-ups; orderly history-taking is key to diagnosis. Sam's approach was far from orderly and Hansen, whose job is to supervise and teach the practice of medicine and validate the findings of his young charges failed on all three counts. Even his billing is suspect.

It should not be concluded that an exhaustive history and a

comprehensive examination of all body systems by attendings and trainees are a realistic expectation in today's teaching hospitals. Nevertheless, at a minimum, the offending organ system deserves the utmost scrutiny. Subtle findings clinching diagnoses often will be detected by a physician with the attitude of a Sherlock Holmes. With his first patient on Medicine, Sam cannot be expected to function like the redoubtable detective, but his supervisor is also an arrogant, insensitive role model. A person like this is fast becoming a doctor who is "often wrong, but never in doubt." Even if Mr. O'Reilly does have acute pancreatitis, in the end, Hansen's haste and superficial approach will eventually hurt someone. What that team needed was an attending!

The implication that many teaching attendings only cursorily supervise their trainees would be unfair. Nevertheless, billing pressures, patient volume, committees, and the desire to return home to family are real temptations to cut corners in education, patient care, and charges for services rendered. Such a harried existence cannot be particularly satisfying or intellectually challenging. Can burnout be far behind?

The more pressing question is this: "Is casual supervision of trainees by attending physicians unethical?" Most often defined as "not morally correct," there are troubling synonyms such as "unprincipled," "unconscionable," and "iniquitous." Flawed though we may be, most of us attendings are not intentionally immoral as we supervise. We want the best for our patients and students; however, affirming a young doctor's examination without verifying the normal or abnormal findings reported may hurt them and their patients. For example, the all-too-often copied-and-pasted phrase, "No murmurs, gallops, or rubs" has begun to replace heart failure's third and acute myocardial infarction's fourth heart sounds. It is the special third-year resident who can even recognize these gallops and teach his or her students.

Among the other endangered species in modern teaching hospitals are the attending or trainee with an ophthalmoscope. In 2015, approximately 17% to 24% of all emergencies for patients older than age 45 were in diabetics.[2] A similar percentage of all patients hospitalized in the United States are diabetics.[3,4] More than one-third have diabetic retinopathy, often vision threatening cases.[5] As such, a perfunctory declaration in a diabetic patient that the HEENT (head, eyes, ears, nose, and throat) examination is

"WNL" could mean, in part, "We Never Looked." In my experience, many erstwhile attendings not only verified our findings as interns, but also expected us before rounds to have personally reviewed the films and the pathology, hematology, or microbiology slides that generated some crucial report. We were embarrassed if we had not, but soon appreciated that actually seeing cells from our patients immediately produced in us new levels of understanding of their diseases and occasionally re-directed the workup.

There are many excellent clinicians among us with the perspicacity to pass on knowledge and skills to our young people. Unfortunately, our focus is increasingly directed to a computer screen and less on them and our patients. With the click of a mouse, we can paste saved, templated, maximum-reimbursement endorsements of a house officer's note on the electronic medical record. This may satisfy our hospital and our department chair, but what about our consciences when it was, we who never looked?

It is time to trust, but verify what trainees report to us. Trainees are hungry to learn and emulate our skills at history-taking and physical diagnosis, interpreting films, and prowess with the microscope. When we uncover a clue they missed that clinches a diagnosis, it is burned into their memories. Moreover, solving the puzzle with them reinforces our own learning, helps keep our enthusiasm high, and burnout remote. These young people are especially tuned-in to our example, and they will pass it on to their students and to thousands of patients we will never meet— anonymous giving of the highest order.

References

1.   Hampton JR, Harrison MJ, Mitchell JR, et al. Relative contributions of history-taking, physical examination, and laboratory investigation to diagnosis and management of medical outpatients. Br Med J 1975; 2:486–489.

2. McEwen LN, Herman WH. Health care utilization and costs of diabetes. In Diabetes in America. 3rd ed. Bethesda, MD: Division of Diabetes, Endocrinology, and Metabolic Diseases of the National Institute of Diabetes and Digestive and Kidney Diseases, National Institutes of Health; 2018: chapter 40.

3. Hall MJ, Rui P, Schwartzman A. Emergency department visits by patients aged 45 and over with diabetes: United States, 2015. NCHS Data Brief 2018;(301):1–8.

4. Tomlin AM, Tilyard MW, Dovey SM, et al. Hospital admissions in diabetic and non-diabetic patients: a case-control study. Diabetes Res Clin Pract 2006; 73:260–267.

5. Lee R, Wong TY, Sabanayagam C. Epidemiology of diabetic retinopathy, diabetic macular edema and related vision loss. Eye Vision (Lond) 2015; 2:17.

Permanent resident

John F. Fisher MD

Medical Education Online, 2016, 21: 31160

Responsibility has always been my best teacher and she began her tutorial in January of 1968 on my first clinical rotation as a third-year medical student at the Medical College of Virginia (MCV) of Virginia Commonwealth University--Medicine at the McGuire VA Medical Center in Richmond, VA. I didn't yet know how to draw blood or start an i.v., but I was assigned to be the 'doctor' for five patients my first morning on the ward. I say ward because that's what it was: an open ward of what must have been 20 patients. The two interns who were on my team were assigned the rest of the patients and the medicine resident supervised them and 'defended' my five from me. Some of these veterans certainly deserved an additional purple heart aside from the ones they were awarded in WW I for the multiple battle wounds I inflicted on their upper extremities prior to discharge. I don't doubt that many of the patients stuck with (and by) me as their doctor suffered post-traumatic stress disorder or battle fatigue as it was called in those days. Nonetheless, on attending rounds, when we got to my patients, I alone had to report on the events of the past 24 hours and the pertinent physical findings and live or die by what I said. The attendings, two of them, patiently suffered through my disorganized and diffuse presentations and verified my amateurish physical exam with seasoned skill and aplomb--and skepticism. On one instance, they were quick to ask me if I had noticed the ghostly-white mucosal pallor and heard the loud S4 in one of my hypertensive, very dark, African-American patients. Only moments before, I had proudly proclaimed my success in bringing his blood pressure under good control with methyldopa. Triumph became despair in an instant. At this early stage in my career, my physical exam skills were only sufficient to confidently state that the patient's heart was present. The association of a fourth heart sound with hypertension I had read about in sophomore year, but William Osler re-incarnated I was not. My heart sank further as they flipped to the lab section of the bedside, aluminum-bound chart. I had overlooked his hemoglobin of 5 gm/dL in the admission labs. Thankfully, my resident had already ordered two units of blood for him before rounds unbeknownst to me. He 'had the patients' backs, but not mine. I died that day on rounds and I came back to haunt the team many more times, but responsibility was quickly making inroads in my education. Happily, by the end of that three-month rotation my supervisors noticed it. My next rotation was a month-long experience in general medicine at a community hospital on the eastern shore of Virginia. There were two bright and charismatic internists supervising me and my student partner. We had two weeks with each physician, working up all new patients and making morning rounds, presenting all the events of the previous day. I could sense that my presentations were just barely beginning to sound like those of the house staff at the VA the previous three months. We were on-call every other night. Especially at night or whenever our supervising doctors were not in the hospital or over in their private offices a few blocks away, the nurses on any floor would call us first about any patient issue. Both of our supervisors expected us to examine the patient, decide what to do, and call them only if we were lost. We were their 'residents' and the ward clerks and nurses carried out our written and verbal orders and the two physicians countersigned them at some time before the patients' discharges. Consequently, I quickly got pretty confident in ordering MOM 30 cc qhs prn; chloral hydrate 500 mg po qhs prn; 2 L of nasal O_2; clear-liquid and 2-g sodium diets; chest radiographs; and CBCs, electrolytes, and blood glucoses; EKGs; and sputum and urine cultures. The pages of the PDR and Lange's Current Medical Diagnosis and Treatment of 1968 became 'dog-eared' from my constant looking things up to avoid hurting a patient or giving my attendings any idea I couldn't handle the pressure or was inept. For much of this 'residency' I didn't need to pester them about minor issues, but I knew my limits and called on them if I felt I had arrived at my own level of incompetence, which was daily. Another valuable lesson was being learned--recognizing when I needed help. Once again, responsibility was shaping me from what had begun three months ago as a hapless figure in a short, white coat into someone just beginning to have a semblance of reasonable judgment at the bedside of a sick patient.

The OB-GYN clinical clerkship at St. Philip Hospital on the MCV campus was the responsibility rotation of a lifetime. My roommate, life-long friend, and the person with the surname just ahead of mine on the class roster, Pasquale Finelli, and I shared every-other-night call in Labor and Delivery. There were so many mothers in active labor every night that the house officers could not possibly deliver all of their babies without the help of Pat and me. I am forever grateful for the saintly patience of the L & D nurses as they talked me through each step of my first few deliveries. They had no other choice—the resident and interns were busy with problems of their own in other rooms with less straight-forward cases. There was a lot of hollering on that floor from primigravidas in pain and anxiety, from hurried doctors under stress, and from nurses scrutinizing the women who were effaced and dilating hoping to alert the resident the name and bed location of the woman who needed to be delivered next and trying to avoid a precipitous 'visit from the stork' in the bed. Cat-napping on a gurney at 3:00 AM was typically the only sleep we got and was especially likely to be interrupted by a call from a nurse like, 'Gravida nine ready to go'. Many of these experienced mothers could have delivered their own baby, but they were inexplicably re-assured by my presence in gown, gloves, and mask.

Nevertheless, my learning curve and my fondness for those women and their babies skyrocketed and I felt myself becoming a bone fide doctor with real clinical judgment. Responsibility strikes again.

The added pressure and need for such judgment became even more acute in caring for kids as I began my internship at the Children's Hospital of the University of Cincinnati. Naively, I had ranked Cincinnati Children's first solely because it was in the beloved city of my boyhood. I had no idea it was and still is one of the best pediatric facilities in the world. Given my zero perspective of academic medicine at the time, I am shocked, but grateful they took me. I had to be at the bottom of their rank list.

On July 1, I began my 'baptism by fire'. I had already survived an on-call schedule of 36-on, 12-off on the eastern shore of Virginia and in the delivery suite at MCV, but that was for a month. Here, I was to spend every other night, largely awake, in the bowels of the hospital for eight months of the year. The schedule for the junior assistant resident and senior assistant resident were the same as mine and the chief resident was on-call every night--God help him. My attendings had done the same and genuinely believed that the main disadvantage of every-other-night call was that one missed the opportunity to learn on half the patients. 'Welcome to real doctoring!', I thought.

A former camp counselor, I loved the kids, but nostalgically I remembered being very happy taking care of the old vets at the McGuire VA too. These heroes of another era were so appreciative of even the smallest kindness a doctor could show them. As a consequence, in starting out my career at Cincinnati Children's, my intention was to become board-certified in both pediatrics and internal medicine. There was no Med-Peds residency as yet, and no time to reminisce or think about that. I was strapped to a wooden plank heading for a buzz saw in this internship. I never met the hospital operator, but I grew to hate the poor woman. She was probably a very sweet person with a pretty home and a nice family. Her voice on the overhead speakers was not at all strident. Indeed, remembering it in a detached, objective way, it was rather delicate and soothing. But every other night, seemingly all night long, the halls resounded incessantly with, 'Doctor Fisher, call 293' (the extension number for the emergency room). Each overhead page meant another child was to be admitted to my service.

One fateful night of call, in the wee small hours of the morning I was in the midst of evaluating the 12 sick kids (including one with diabetic ketoacidosis) already admitted to me, when her dulcet page portended the admission of a second child with ketoacidosis. I ducked into an alcove somewhere and privately cried for a moment until I could catch my second wind. The head nurse, Ms. Pauline Heymann, a kind, stately, sixtyish woman in her crisp, white uniform and cap and white oxfords spotted me in my despair and patted my shoulder gently and understandingly. Her words of encouragement are long forgotten, but I thank her for helping me survive that night. Responsibility this time was ramming my clinical education down my throat--with a cruel, rigid scope. My supervisors were empathetic and supportive. They really did have my back, but they expected me to 'man up', make careful decisions, and take good care of my patients. For example, if one of my admissions had been a patient of one of our hematology attendings and I hadn't personally reviewed the patient's Wright-stained blood film, he would chew me up and spit me out on morning rounds. He was right, but responsibility had jagged teeth at times. I still treasure all those wonderful kids and that world-class faculty, but I abandoned the idea of being double-boarded, left the kids behind, and switched to internal medicine the next year.

Resident call on the UC medical service was every third night. My fellow house staff whined about the frequency, but I thought I was on vacation! Now for the first time, I was in charge of the team. Our unspoken commitment was to protect our attending, let him (in those patriarchal days) teach three days a week, and call only when we truly did not know what to do after rifling through the pages of Harrison's or Cecil's textbooks of internal medicine. One call night I was feeling pretty perspicacious as I made the diagnosis of Addison's disease in a tan-skinned, wasted, hypotensive ex-soldier with hyponatremia and hyperkalemia who presented to the VA emergency room. Unfortunately, I had carelessly glossed over his history of rheumatic fever as a child and because of his classic 'small, quiet heart' hadn't heard any murmur on exam. I found a recent article on treatment and began fluids and hydrocortisone without calling our attending, fully confident to receive the accolades due to me on rounds the next day. Having read up on the disease, I was 'loaded for bear' and delivered a rather theatrical presentation the next morning.

My attending politely listened, examined the patient, and then questioned me as to why he had the early signs of congestive heart failure with an S3, a loud murmur of mitral regurgitation, and bibasilar rales. Red-faced, I quickly realized that with my steroids and saline I had volume-expanded a patient with significant valvular heart disease. Fortunately, my patient fared well in spite of me. Tinsley Harrison I was not, but I was still learning by having been given responsibilities and the successes and failures which go with it. My residency was interrupted by a stint in the US Navy as a Flight Surgeon, countless flight physicals, and the occasional patients whom I medicated or sutured when on-call, but I returned three years later to finish me medicine residency. The faces of the interns and students had gotten younger, but my routine and the tasks were the same--work up patients and write notes (WP), teach the younger folks (T), read (R), make work rounds (WR) and attending rounds (AR), and go to conferences (C). I didn't fully understand academic medicine until I began my fellowship in infectious diseases which required scholarly output for the first time as well as quality patient care. Once again, we ID fellows ran the consult service with cameo appearances by the attendings who were more focused on their research and endorsed our notes with a quick slash of the pen. I hadn't changed my stripes an iota. It was still-- WP, T, R, WR, AR, and C.

Detailed faculty documentation requirements began in earnest with the birth of diagnosis-related groups (DRGs) (1) at about the same time I arrived at the Medical College of Georgia (of Augusta University) as a green assistant professor. I was expecting to follow in the footsteps of my attendings-of-old--teaching young people, affixing my surname on progress notes, writing papers, and letting the residents run the service like I had. Instead, billing patients at the right level of care rather abruptly became my most important function. The federal government now demanded more written visibility from me-- longer notes, requisite numbers of responses of the patients to my review of their organ systems, and proof of body parts examined--or it wouldn't pay my hospital.

Insurance companies soon followed the lead of the Feds. Resident, intern, and student notes became inconsequential. At one point in our hospital, attending physicians were required to hand-write a complete history and physical examination on each new admission and re-iterate salient features of patients' daily progress. I found myself 'back in the saddle' of my residency again. It wasn't long before I began receiving passive-aggressive communications about missing components of my notes from chart reviewers employed by our billing office. Each of these oversights had to be fixed before discharge. Because others had begun their notes one line below mine--the one with the missing elements-- I developed a new talent at cramming legibly in the margin and, with up- or down-arrows, between lines. Moreover, despite my lack of ability and interest in the business of medicine, I was given an assignment that none of my medical training had prepared me for: billing my patients for each encounter at the correct Current Procedural Terminology (CPT) code of the Healthcare Common Procedure Coding System (HCPCS) (2)--checking boxes on a sheet in each chart labeled 99221-3 or 99231-3. Identifying the date and the level of care I rendered, the hospital billed patients accordingly in my name. This task couldn't be done during or immediately after morning rounds with the residents and students because of noon conferences. Under pain of excommunication, I had to find time to do it sometime that afternoon. Naturally, my time-window frequently did not correspond to whether the patients and their charts were on the ward or off to some diagnostic or therapeutic procedure or already discharged. As one might anticipate, many billing opportunities were missed in this system and led to more dunning, delinquency messages. I doubt if I was alone in this struggle and sensed that, unlike my revered predecessors in academic medicine, attending physicians were fast becoming the enemy of hospital administrators and chairs of departments. The electronic medical record has solved the cramming problem with a mere keystroke for us attendings once we become facile at logging on, finding the offending note, and adding the required ad valorem language. However, notification of a delinquency often occurs days to weeks after the patient encounter making the truthfulness of these mercenary addenda dependent on remote recall. Curiously, many of the ones I have read written by other faculty are word-for-word like previous entries. I hesitate to use that hackneyed 'p' word, but there has been an unequivocal paradigm shift in academic medicine today. Fear of litigation and multi-million-dollar settlements resulting from medical errors by trainees is undoubtedly one of the driving forces behind the shift.

Nevertheless, most teaching hospital CEOs will cite patient safety and outcomes for strictly enforcing the Accreditation Council for Graduate Medical Education's guidelines for reduced work hours and curtailed autonomy for residents. This is despite the fact that definitive data showing increased mortality for traditional models of patient care and graded, increasing responsibility for trainees are lacking. Indeed, the recent Study to Understand Nighttime Staffing Effectiveness in a Tertiary ICU (SUNSET-ICU) actually showed that in-house residents with access to fellows and attendings by phone produced the same outcomes as staffing the ICU with board-certified, critical-care specialists supervising residents at night (3). Increased supervision and its unproven effect on patient safety should be studied to determine if this is the most effective and efficient way to improve outcomes (4). Attending physicians in many academic medical centers are writing fewer papers and in real danger of 'burnout' from an increasing workload and decreasing job satisfaction (5). They truly have become the 'fall guys' (and gals) with all the responsibility. The young ones are getting their first taste of it immediately after they complete their specialty training rather than from the get-go and it will at long last begin to teach them as it taught me. Unfortunately, it will teach them less about taking care of patients. Those of us who are 'long-in-the-tooth' have been residents since the first day we appeared on the wards.

References

1. Russell GI. Terminology. In: Alexander BD, ed. Fundamentals of health law 1. 5th ed. Albany, NY: LexisNexis Matthew Bender; 2011, p. 12.

2. American Medical Association. Current procedural terminology. 1st ed. American Medical Association.

3. Kerlin MP, Small DS, Cooney E, Fuchs BD, Bellini LM, Mikkelsen ME, et al. A randomized trial of nighttime physician staffing in an intensive care unit. N Engl J Med 2013; 368: 2201_9.

4. Halpern SD, Detsky AS. Graded autonomy in medical education _ Managing things that go bump in the night. N Engl J Med 2014; 370: 1086_9.

5. Shanafelt TD, West CP, Sloan JA, Novotny PJ, Poland GA, Menaker R, et al. Career fit and burnout among academic faculty. Arch Intern Med 2009; 169: 990_5.

Where have you Gone, Sherlock Holmes?

John F. Fisher MD

Clinical Microbiology Open Access 2013. 2:e114

Abstract

Dr. Jack House is a fictitious infectious disease fellow who has been allowed to practice superficial and potentially harmful patient evaluations because attending physicians are too busy to adequately supervise him. His consultations on four critically ill patients have been performed in haste and recommendations have been based on faulty reasoning with inadequate data. He has failed to incorporate microscopy into his thought process and his clinical notes are overly brief, poorly written, and call for inappropriately broad-spectrum antimicrobial therapy. His consultation style is contrasted with real examples of patients who were evaluated by an infectious disease consultant who relied heavily on clinical exam and microscopic findings to arrive at an accurate diagnosis and to give recommendations for appropriate antimicrobial therapy. The article is a commentary on an increasingly pervasive type of infectious disease practice.

It was November 30th and today his beeper had vibrated so many times that the first signs of a friction burn had developed over the right iliac crest of Jack House MD, first-year ID fellow at Summa Cum Laude University Medical Center. If the beeper had been in his shirt pocket, he might have developed a productive cough. He had already "seen" and scribbled a one-paragraph note on three new consults recommending doripenem plus caspofungin for two of the patients who had some kind of enigmatic, febrile illness. He had successfully fended off six other consults by asking the callers if the patient could be seen tomorrow and whining about being swamped, craftily concealing the fact that another fellow was taking over the service in the AM.

Two of the four patients he reluctantly agreed to evaluate were in the ICU receiving mechanical ventilation. These acutely ill individuals, like many others in his three previous rotations on the consult service, had a tube in every orifice. Both were on contact isolation. Dr. House perfunctorily donned his yellow gown and latex gloves and went into the patients' rooms. He glanced vacantly at their careworn faces and listened with the patients' dedicated stethoscopes through their gowns over the precordial area and the anterior, apical lung regions. Since no attending in his training had ever examined patients in sufficient detail to challenge his physical findings, he had settled in to this exam style with surprisingly little guilt. If pressed, he knew down deep, after these brief patient encounters, he could only honestly certify (1) that the heart and lungs were present and (2) that the patients were on a ventilator even though his note claimed that the lungs were "clear to A & P." His guilt was assuaged to a large degree because that same abbreviation was common to the notes of the junior medical student, medicine resident, and critical care fellow for the past 48 hours on both patients. The pulmonary attending who was the very soul of brevity had "agreed with house staff's findings and treatment plan" each day. Dr. House felt comforted by his assumption that the official laboratory and X-ray findings would tell him all he really needed to know about these patients. He hadn't carried an ophthalmoscope since he was a junior medical student (None of the fellows and medicine residents did either.). The thought of getting a nurse to help him turn the patients to listen to the posterior lung fields and examine for a rash and pressure sores or to obtain a suctioned sputum or urine sample for microscopy never even entered his head. Furthermore, he had to get the notes written before rounds if he wanted to get to his lucrative moonlighting job by 5:30PM.

Dr. House made it a practice each day to review the *Sanford Guide to Antimicrobial Therapy* just before attending rounds relative to all new consults and he did very well on standardized exams. Furthermore, he was "hail 'fellow' well met," had movie-star good looks, and had played middle linebacker for the state university as an undergraduate. As expected, he was very popular with attendings of either gender, but not with the other ID fellows to whom he turned over the service.

His third patient was on 9 West Medical Ward with a refractory community-acquired pneumonia whose sputum had yielded only *Candida albicans* in culture. In his thinking process, since the Microbiology Laboratory had reported that the sample contained many neutrophils, the yeast must have undoubtedly been real and needed treating. Dr. House reasoned that he should once again recommend doripenem in addition to the echinocandin on the outside chance that the patient's probable *Candida* pneumonia was part of a polymicrobial infection which included *Pseudomonas* or anaerobes. Caspofungin was advised because reports are rampant about the increasing resistance of yeast to fluconazole. As far as going to the Microbiology Laboratory to review the Gram's stain from the patient's current sputum sample or original admission sample, forget that. He had never had an ID attending in his first three rotations on the consult service who told him that this exercise might provide useful diagnostic information even if the smear revealed no organisms. He would have been dumfounded if one of his ID attendings had asked him if he had looked at a wet mount, AFB smear, or Wright stain of the sputum samples. However, this wasn't likely since all of his supervisors were under 40 and very busy in their laboratories and he knew they would sign off on his doripenem plus caspofungin cocktail.

For the last consult Dr. House planned to see before attending rounds that day, he recommended six weeks of daptomycin plus rifampin for a patient with a spinal cord injury and, according to the nurse, "a nasty looking, stage-three, sacral pressure sore." Once again he confirmed that this patient's heart and lungs were present, but Dr. House did not take the dressing down from the decubitus ulcer and check with sterile gloves for the presence of exposed bone, undermined wound margins, fascial integrity, and malodorous discharge. However, swabs of the ulcer had yielded VRE and this organism, especially if it involved bone, he felt must be treated for a long time. His handwriting on the three notes was so scrawled that it took the consulting residents longer to read the note than Dr. House took to evaluate the patients. They were never able to decipher whose signature and beeper number was on the consult form, but fortunately they were able to make out Doribax®+Cancidas®, and Cubicin®. Dr. House, like all residents and faculty, used trade names because the generic names were just too hard to pronounce. Ironically, Summa Cum Laude University Medical Center was one of the first medical schools to outlaw pharmaceutical representatives on campus. They needn't have. The constant use of these Madison Avenueconceived proprietary names and many others besides (Zosyn®, Rocephin®, Levaquin®, Primaxin®, Reyataz®, Presista®, Valtrex®, and Truvada®) do the selling in absentia for the reps. The junior medical students were just beginning to master the trade names after five months on the wards and a difficult second year with generics and structure-activity relationships. Most residents and fellows remember what class of antimicrobials these agents belong to, but little else. Dr. House's cramming for a few minutes each day with the *Sanford Guide* helped him appear to them a walking encyclopedia of antimicrobial therapeutics. Even his ID attendings noted on his evaluations that his fund of knowledge right down to correct dosages of medications for renal insufficiency was precocious for his level of training. No mention was ever made of the clarity or quality of his consult notes.

That Dr. House has no genuine interest in precise infectious disease diagnosis or in-depth understanding and judicious use of antibiotics are symptoms of a poorly encapsulated neoplasm which has metastasized throughout the United States. However, the blame cannot be completely placed on him or our other young trainees. It must be shared. To borrow from Walt Kelly's Pogo, "We have met the enemy and he is us." When we don't inspire our charges to perform careful histories, "world-class" physical examinations, and microscopic analysis of clinical specimens or demonstrate the exhilaration and constant challenge of correctly managing patients with infectious diseases, the fault is ours. We should not only inspire, but expect this pursuit of excellence and trust them to carry it out. That is, trust, but verify. Needed or not, broad-spectrum anti-bacterials and anti-fungals would be effective for most common bacteria and yeast and the fairly frequent clinical improvement of the patients who receive them reinforces their inappropriate use. The physicians who prescribe them are in most instances never challenged on their reasoning for ordering them and rotate off the service or graduate long before the unit has to deal with an outbreak of multi-drug-resistant organisms. When education committees of our societies can honestly conclude that teaching microscopic skills to ID fellows is not a worthwhile, practical endeavor and is not a part of the Program Requirements of the Accreditation Council on Graduate Medical Education for our specialty, something has gone seriously awry.

Whether or not the Occupational Safety and Health Administration sanctions our interpretation of microscopic smears and wet mounts, we should continue to use these valuable tools to assist us in our decision-making. Despite the fact that in many instances microscopy is not helpful and we are forced to employ broad-spectrum agents in critically ill patients, there are frequent occasions when a meticulous exam and the use of the microscope has been pivotal in arriving at a diagnosis and treatment strategy. Here are three examples:

Case 1

A man with COPD was admitted to the hospital for an acute exacerbation and intubated for respiratory failure. Imaging showed bilateral alveolar infiltrates. Despite broad-spectrum antibiotics, the pneumonia worsened. An infectious disease physician was consulted. Careful physical exam showed diffuse rales in both posterior lung fields. Gram, AFB, and Wright stain of bloody sputum donepersonally by the consultant disclosed no organisms. Wet mount showed numerous larvae of *Strongyloides stercoralis*.

Case 2

A woman in her 20s with advanced AIDS was admitted for high fever and rigors. A careful system review revealed no pulmonary, urinary tract, or other symptoms. A thorough physical examination was unhelpful. A complete blood count showed a moderate anemia and thrombocytopenia. Bone marrow aspirate and biopsy was recommended by the ID consultant and performed by the Hematology/Oncology service. Smears and special stains were completed by pathology technicians late in the afternoon and would not be evaluated until the next workday by a pathologist. Because the patient's condition became unstable, hospital security was called to allow access to the Pathology Laboratory after hours. The ID consultant reviewed the Gomori-methenamine silver stain of the bone marrow and found several, small, budding yeast consistent with *Histoplasma capsulatum*. Amphotericin B was started and by morning, the patient was much improved. Bone marrow culture yielded *H. capsulatum* many days later.

Case 3

The patient was a renal transplant recipient with productive cough and a pulmonary infiltrate unresponsive to broad-spectrum antibiotics. Sputum cultures were pending. The official interpretation of the Gram stain by the Microbiology Laboratory indicated that the sputum was adequate, but no microorganisms were noted. The physicians caring for the patient consulted Infectious Disease. The ID attending reviewed the aforementioned Gram stain and found many examples of faintly staining, beaded, Gram-positive, filamentous rods consistent with *Nocardia* spp which later grew in culture. The official report was corrected and the patient received trimethoprim-sulfamethoxazole and recovered.

Infectious disease colleagues from all over the world trained in microscopy, if queried, could cite many similar examples where our skills at the bedside and with the microscope made the difference in the survival of a sick patient. It is time we demanded the recognition that a thorough history, a meticulous physical examination, and microscopic analysis are our "stock-in-trade" and that they are critical to the practice of clinical microbiology and infectious disease. We owe this to the next generation of practitioners of our beloved specialty. If we fail in this endeavor, Dr. House and his ilk will take our places. They will always be in a hurry; they will deal with patients very cavalierly and superficially; they will do little critical thinking; and many of their patients will die without a diagnosis. They will drive up the cost of health care by treating culture results rather than patients; and, sadly, they will burn out because their brand of medicine is neither challenging nor satisfying. However, if we are successful in passing on our timeless practice style to these bright and idealistic young men and women, we will have given anonymous gifts to them and to thousands of patients we will never meet.

Lecturing To Medical Students--Time To Throw In The Towel?

John F. Fisher MD

The classroom was designed to accommodate 225 students. They were all there at Orientation excited and ready to become new doctors. But today is the fourth week of posted and video-recorded basic science lectures and now attendance had dwindled to 30 or so "gunners." Can one blame the students when the first lecture is at 8:00AM, parking is a big problem at the medical school, and it's a much more efficient use of time to insert ear buds and listen alone to the recording? They can and will fast-forward most professors or rewind as necessary and make notes on their computer screen while eating their wonuts and drinking dark-roast from their three-pillow orthopneic position in bed.

It may be time to find a better way for faculty to reach med students than by reading bullets to them from behind the podium or in the dark from slide templates they fancy to be quite avant-guarde. Unfortunately, many of their bullets are in Times New Roman 10 font, unreadable beyond the first two rows, and are long, complete sentences replete with articles and conjunctions. It would never occur to them that those who came gunning for every exam point are only half-listening, distracted and trying to find which bullet the professor is presently referring to since many are glossed over as the teacher rushes to get through all the slides. At first blush, the lecturer seems knowledgeable enough to the students as the slides are recited to them verbatim. After all, they know next-to-nothing themselves about the subject and this is a specialist talking, err…reading to them. In reality, it is mostly a ruse because this or that assistant professor may have appropriated some genuine expert's slide lecture on this subject from the internet and adapted it to his or her own ingeniously creative design talents. If the electricity went out, they could never give an organized, extemporaneous summary of their subject because they need to read those bullets.

Irrespective of the pastels of the slide background and the bullets which march in from varied angles to the sound of snare drums or locomotives, the lecturers often read in a 10-decibel monotone which certainly does not reach the last row. Those who do garner teaching awards year after year simply have read each of their bullets with great vocal inflection and modulation, and above all, enthusiasm.

In fairness, many professors are overwrought with patient responsibilities, teaching rounds, and the all-important notes to write on the electronic medical record which generates their salary. Many PhDs are trying to meet grant application deadlines for sheer survival. Teaching has to be an afterthought for many. Furthermore, a bulleted lecture doubles as a good handout with no more extra work than a computer stroke. Moreover, students assume this is the norm for medical education since they saw the beginnings of this in middle school, high school, and college and some will even whine if a lecturer dares to stray from this tired format.

It's time for the bulleted lecture to be greatly overhauled or "deep-sixed" forever. If this is to be the standard, why have lectures at all in the curriculum? If anyone claims I'm referring to the hackneyed term, 'paradigm shift', I'll deny it (I also vow to never utter the word, 'robust' except in derision). Lectures should be _events_ at least partially resembling _TED talks_ especially in length. They should be full of non-copyrighted clinical images of a concept or, alternatively, hand-drawn or professionally created, which can be explained in the speaker's own words. Line graphs, bar graphs, and pie charts should no longer be downloaded from a journal article along with their complicated legends and hard-to-read data points. Such graphs only cause a frustrating search for the title of the ordinate and abscissa before the professor moves to the next slide. Instead, the teaching points will be made in a simplified graph and summarized so that listeners can recognize at a glance what data are being shown. If bullets are employed, each is a word or a short phrase in a bold font (16+) like Arial which the teacher and the audience can take-in at a glance. The lecturer will then be forced to clearly understand the subject to competently explain images, graphs, or short bullets. As all who prepare lectures from this kind of preparation know, "The teacher learns the most."

Students may even begin to come to lecture early because they want to find a parking space to listen to a talented and knowledgeable educator who speaks with the lights up whom they can see. He or she is part ham-actor who can be heard in the back of the lecture hall and able to explain the images in fairly simple terms and, best of all, does so with enthusiasm and passion. This teacher interacts with the audience and quizzes them while keeping it light and minimally intimidating. This professor never distracts the audience by walking and talking simultaneously. Rather, the lecturer moves silently with purpose, grabbing attention, while walking toward one part of the audience. The teacher then stops and makes direct eye contact with one person in the audience. Holding that eye contact, a teaching point is made before looking directly at another student to make a second point. Following this interaction, the teacher moves again silently to the center or opposite side of the audience, stops, and repeats the technique. Students will then believe that the professor is lecturing personally to them.

Promotion through the academic ranks in medical schools requires state-of-the-art patient care, a love of science, scholarship, and service to the institution. We are advanced with the designation's assistant, associate, or full professor. But too many of us are not really _professing_ judging by the present goings-on in the lecture hall. Wasn't one of our reasons for choosing an academic career because we enjoy teaching young people the art and science of medicine? We have a unique opportunity to give anonymously to patients we will never meet. For some of us the impact of our lectures on these patients will be our only gift to them. Too many of the gifts we currently are offering to both our students and their patients should be labeled, "Return to Sender."

Stop Being So Serious, John Fisher!

Lecturing for Industry—Death by PowerPoint®

John F. Fisher MD

South Med J 2009; 102: 133-4

In a cramped antechamber with noisy, sliding glass doors just off the main dining room of a trendy Italian restaurant, a few physicians, a few more hospital pharmacists, two nurse clinicians, and a medical technologist mill about in several uncomfortable groups waiting for the "educational program" to begin. The representative of the drug company sponsoring this soiree has hand-picked each invitee because of their membership on the Pharmacy and Therapeutics Committee of one of the local hospitals. Rather vacuous small talk and feigned laughter are heard as each person jockeys for a spot to stand out of the way of the bustling waiters taking beer, wine, and mixed-drink orders amid the several large, round tables for eight. The LCD projector is at the ready, but its tippy, jerry-rigged perch and the unwieldy, finger-pinching, retractable screen and cardboard lectern only add to the clutter and block easy access to a table via the front of the room. While the lectern is equipped with an unnecessary microphone and a laser pointer, there is no room for the speaker's laptop, which is plugged into the nearest outlet (in the next room) and rests precariously on a cushioned chair and will fall if any guest or waiter even moves the already taut extension cord. As a result, the lecturer must not only be cautious, but half-genuflect to advance the slides. The speaker is an Assistant Professor of Infectious Disease who is struggling to meet his new mortgage and private school tuition and needs the honorarium from this dinner lecture. He has successfully completed the online training that the founder of the feast requires for his spot on the regional speaker's list. The speaker is dressed in the traditional blue blazer and khaki trousers, but his tie is a little avant-garde with its myriad of chartreuse koalas on a light blue background. He secretly hopes it will fashionably convey to his audience his love of all living things and knowledge of the world. However, this message is doomed not only by the choice of colors, but by its rather untoward and bulky Windsor knot—not to mention the unbuttoned collar on one side. To put it not too unkindly, the tie just misses.

As the speaker is introduced by the rep, the room is dimmed and the talk begins with the waiters dodging the light from the projector, stepping over the extension cord, and audibly whispering to the now-seated group to take pasta and additional drink orders. The host pharmaceutical company has armed the speaker with a thumb drive containing 70 Powerpoint® slides. Each slide averages 25 bullet points, many of which cannot be read from the back of even these tight quarters. The font chosen by the company is unbolded Times New Roman 10—not what the fledgling specialist ordinarily employs for medical school lectures, but he is forbidden under pain of excommunication to add anything of his own to the talk or remove anything from it. The few slides which are not bulleted have complicated 3D bar graphs, which are poorly labeled with the key to the colors off to the side. While the several people in the audience who are red-green colorblind will see each bar as a dull shade of brown, none in the small audience, not even those with the color perception of a Kandinsky or Mondrian, could understand the graph anyway. In any event, they were sifting through their salads for one more crouton. Fearful of arrest by an armed member of the FDA or Pharmaceutical Research and Manufacturers of America security forces, the young specialist dutifully reads each bulleted sentence on each slide without missing one. The items recited verbatim are not really bullet points, but whole sentences replete with unnecessary conjunctions and articles. There are no summary slides, no cartoons, no humorous asides or anecdotes, and not even a glimpse of the young doctor's personality. Conspicuously absent is any mention of any competitors' products. Because the lecturer must stick to the script, his back is half-turned to a half-interested audience. With the help of the red dot from the laser pointer bouncing slightly erratically and tremulously over each word on each slide, they follow his recitation as much as they would be if the venue werea karaoke bar. The audience's lip movements and chewing often move in-sync with him as he reads. If they turn away from the screen for a bite of their meal, they can quickly catch up—unless the speaker absentmindedly points the laser to their maculae.

But the wine is decent and the pasta is good and the waiter never allows their water level to fall below three-quarters full. And the rattling ice is a welcome distraction that breaks up the monotony of having someone read technical "medicalese" aloud. However, the two glasses of wine (or the three Heinekens) combined with the veal scaloppini are beginning to take effect by slide number 58. Eyes begin blinking infrequently and glazing over as the speaker drones on with his soporific monotone without taking a breath and without emphasis or any other modulation of his just barely audible voice. Oblivious to the effect this lecture is having on the others in the room, the pharmaceutical rep continues to nod enthusiastically and knowingly on each bullet point. Since the room is dark and the speaker's back is turned and he is concentrating so hard on the scripted bullets, he is not insulted by the retired general practitioner whose chin has abruptly come to rest on his chest. For the past 15 minutes, the retiree has been fighting sleep desperately, almost suffering a severe whiplash injury on several occasions. With the numerous, sharp osteophytes in the old doctor's cervical spine, it is nothing short of a miracle he has not been pithed during the presentation. But let him have his sweet repose, since he has not understood a word anyway. His only hope for arousal from early REM might have been the mention of sulfisoxazole, polymyxin B, or lincomycin. An ever-widening circle of wetness from the drool escaping from his open mouth now begins to darken his tan Hawaiian shirt just above the pocket. When he awakens, he will find that the logo pens he stuffed in it earlier are now soaked. Mercifully, this unfortunate occurrence, coupled with the early faint traces of the old man's snoring, signal to the speaker and the rep that he and most likely the whole audience have had enough—all but the stout, single, medical technologist who has been watching the young lecturer's every move, hoping to catch his eye and return his look with her best alluring expression. She especially likes that tie.

In the final analysis, the only beneficiaries of the presentation have been the speaker (once he has completed his expense voucher and waited six weeks for processing), the attendees, who paid little attention to the lecture and were really there for the pasta (even if this meal satisfied their entire monthly quota of cholesterol and was eaten in virtual darkness), and the new Italian restaurant who reaped exorbitant profits from the affair. The waiters sentenced to serve this dinner made their usual two dollars per hour but got the short-shrift for the evening because there were no tips. Those who tried to pay attention and learn something had a commercial read to them from a young gun—a hired one at that. Ironically, in the drug company's agreement with Pharmaceutical Research and Manufacturers of America to avoid any appearance of impropriety, a tedious advertisement has been recited to the audience and the only one who has been fooled is the medical technologist whose heart is soon to be broken yet again by the physician-speaker's wedding band, which she had failed to spot in the dark.

Lost Weekend in Dover--
Missed the White Cliffs: A Nightmare in Space A Travel

John F. Fisher CAPT USNR (ret.)

*Originally published in *Hackwriters*, August 21, 2017

I headed out in my Honda Pilot for the three-hour trip to Charleston, SC, Air Force Base from my home in Augusta, GA, on a Wednesday morning. I should have heeded the omen—a constant, torrential downpour-- and turned back right then. However, I was determined to get to Leipzig by sometime the next day. I was scheduled to give some lectures in that old German city on-camera for a private educational firm. If I could get on the manifest for an overseas Space A flight in Charleston, not only would I be saving them airfare, but I would be safe in the arms of the military during my flight with little of the hassle of flying commercial. As it happened, I would have welcomed that hassle compared to what was to befall me over the next four days.

Despite limited visibility, the pelting of the rain on my car roof and onto my lap and left sleeve through the open driver-side window, I was able to catch about half of the halting directions from AB (Airman Basic) Sam Gavonovich at the front gate of Charleston AFB. Squinting through sheets of water and with my nose protruding through the steering wheel, I finally located the Passenger Air Terminal. In a moment of arrogant entitlement, since I was a retired Navy captain, I cavalierly commandeered an 'Authorized Parking Only' space as close to the building as possible because I knew the next hundred yards were going to be wet ones. Naturally, my golf umbrella was in the rear compartment of my SUV next to my clubs and I wasn't about to venture outside in this deluge to do anything yet. I still had the ignition on and was mainly contemplating my next move, half-listening to Dr. Laura lambaste a divorced woman with three young children for shacking up with and financially supporting a man she met on-line three months ago. Sanctimoniously happy I didn't need her advice, I decided to act decisively.

In a most ungainly fashion, I urged my decrepit body into the back seat over the headrest to get to my raincoat. I realized at once that a raincoat was not meant to be donned while seated in cramped quarters as I struggled to get my arms into the sleeves. Reaching behind me, I almost dislocated my right shoulder trying to unzip the pouch of my golf bag near the tailgate which contained my golf rain suit. Professional contortionists would have applauded if they could have seen and especially heard my efforts to get my rain apparel on without tearing even my shorts.

Now clad for a monsoon except for my leather loafers which were ruined in the first 50 yards, I sloshed my way into the terminal and up to the reception desk. I knew instantly because of the echoing laughter and idle chatting of two or three Air Force enlisted and no other visible human beings that there would be no flights to Germany or any other city leaving that afternoon. Indeed, the first hop from Charleston to anywhere was to the West Coast in 48 hours. I was courteously directed to the base long-term parking area about a half a mile away. I figured that if I left my car at the AFB, I could rather easily return from Europe to Charleston in 10 days and drive back home.

As I understood it, the Air Force's gigantic C5A Galaxies were home-based in Dover, Delaware—at least they were when I was on active duty in the 1970s. Surely, I thought, if I can get to Dover this afternoon, I could be headed for Europe on one of those big birds maybe even today. Charleston International Airport was only a short, eleven-dollar taxi ride away. I wasn't even discouraged to find out at the American Airlines counter that the closest I could get to Dover from Charleston was to fly to Philadelphia. Since I'd already saved at least $1500 by my plan to travel Space A, the commercial flight to Philadelphia would be most affordable at $564 and a $25 baggage charge. Moreover, the German company would reimburse me for my travel. I could rent a car and drive to Dover, stay in a hotel, and be first-in-line at the Dover AFB Passenger Terminal in the morning and off to Deutschland. Although the first flight to Philadelphia didn't depart until 6:15 PM, that was still the "shank of the evening" to me. I was bound to be driving to Dover by no later than 9:00PM. It turned out to be more like 10:00PM. As unfazed as Don Quixote, I left the airport in Philly in the smallest, compact, $227-car money could rent. The rain I left behind in Charleston caught up with me on I-95S heading for the Dover exit 50 minutes away. Had I brought along a passenger, he would have had a death grip on the door handle and a thrilling ride on that unfamiliar stretch of road which was alive with vehicles traveling too fast for conditions in all lanes. Straining to read the Delaware state road exit signs in the driving rain, I found myself headed west instead of east for only 20 minutes before I noted that the mileage to Dover was increasing rather than decreasing. It was only another six miles to the next exit, but I didn't mind. I'd get the car headed in the right direction in a few minutes and Dover was only 68 miles the other way. I hadn't counted on getting so sleepy and there were no rest stops on that dark road, so I had to really fight it the last 15 miles to get to a busy highway with hotel choices in Dover. I checked into a Hampton Inn for $132.35, found an Appleby's nearby, and was able to order a hamburger just before the kitchen closed.

In my anticipation about the flight tomorrow and the nightly interruptions of a prostate over 70 years-old, I slept fitfully until 5:00AM. One benefit of my insomnia was that I had first choice for the hotel's complimentary breakfast and could leisurely pour my coffee and fill my paper plate with scrambled eggs and bacon without elbowing another guest invading my space and impatiently waiting for his turn. I couldn't return my rental car until 7:30AM, but I got my gear, typed the address into my phone, and the GPS guided me right to the location. After settling up, a very kind Enterprise employee drove me to Dover AFB Passenger Terminal.

I was the first potential passenger on the manifest for a C17 to Ramstein AFB in southwest Germany. I was ready to board, but was told that the plane was scheduled to depart at 1700—10 hours hence. No problem—I had lectures to prepare. Other Space A hopefuls, some active duty with spouses and small children, and some retirees and their wives began to check-in over the course of the morning. Because of heavy cargo, there were only 17 jump seats for passengers on this trip. I learned, with not a little foreboding, that many of these folks had signed up for Space A travel weeks ago and would be given a seat ahead of me. My heart began to pound at 1300 when the roll call began for travelers, starting with active duty personnel and those retirees like me in the order of sign-up. My loud sigh of relief when they called me for seat number 17 must have reverberated through the terminal at 1400. Baggage and Security check-in was to begin at 1600 which went surprisingly smoothly and on-time. I knew in my Naval bones that there had to be a "hurry up and wait" somewhere in this process and there was. We all sat in the boarding area biding our time, contemplating our navels, and watching seemingly endless numbers of huge pallets being painstakingly loaded by forklift onto our aircraft until 1800. Didn't they realize that I had to get to Germany? Finally, we boarded and sat on the shuttle bus until 1830. At last we were driven to the C17. Because I had been an O-6, I was called by name and ceremoniously asked to be first to board the aircraft. Giving my best impression of false humility, I climbed the ladder (steps in Air Force jargon) and located the jump seat, which I mistakenly imagined would be the most comfortable, and strapped in. All 17 of us were seated and given safety instructions over the din of the Pratt and Whitney turbofan engines and we began taxiing at 1930. There was a moment of the usual excitement as we came to a halt when we were number one for take-off (The only other aircraft on the base was another C17 which had been parked there all week). The engines began to roar, only to be brought back to idle a few seconds later. The enlisted airman in-charge then announced that the aircraft's radio had malfunctioned and we had to return to the tarmac. It became 2000 hours when we were shuttled by bus back to the boarding area awaiting the repair of the radio. At 2200 we were told that parts for the radio could not be installed and the flight would be scratched until the same time tomorrow. Roll call would be at 1300 as usual. I was less than thrilled at the prospect of another day in Dover, but I assumed that electrical problems like this were minor and I'd easily be in Germany early Friday morning and hop a train to Leipzig.

This unhappy turn of events forced us 17 "Space-A'ers" to locate places to bed down at the bewitching hour somewhere in Dover, prompting a scurry of cell phone activity and a race for reservations and too few cabs. Finishing dead last in this competition, my ride-to-a-hotel problem was solved by a Navy enlisted retiree whose truck happened to be parked on the base in anticipation of his return from Europe. I accepted his kind offer of a lift to a hotel assuming I could find a vacant one. As he was dressed in Bermuda shorts, knee socks, sneakers, and a loud Hawaiian shirt draped over an enormous 'papa belly', the two of us could not be any more contrasting—or so I thought until his life story began to unfold in conversation. Over a beer in a local tavern he told me he was divorced, had sold all his belongings, paid all his debts, bought a pickup and traveled anywhere he pleased all over the U.S. and the world. He had his Navy retirement check sent electronically to his bank. At night, he located convenient, free parking in whatever city he found himself, and slept in his truck. He belonged to a national health club chain and would go to a local franchise to shower and shave and then, in true Willie Nelson fashion, he was back on the road again. He had apparently lived like this for a year or more. Indeed, on this particular night, he slept in the parking lot of the hotel where I had been able to find a room and, in the morning, drove me back to the Dover AFB Passenger Terminal to finally get on that C17 for Germany.

The schedule for baggage and security check-in was exactly the same as the previous day. In between times there were appetizing trips to the drink and snack machines, a scenic hike to the Commissary, mesmerizing vistas of the tarmac, multiple, pleasant visits to the rest room, and riveting small talk with other passengers. What with these activities, along with staring at the ceiling and changing to a new stick of gum when it began to taste like a rubber washer, the hours simply sped by.

Full of renewed purpose and anticipation at 1830 we were once again shuttled to our C17 and this time I confidently led my troops to their jump seats. Within 30 minutes we were number one for takeoff, roared and shuddered down the runway and at last, aloft. The 100-decibels of the engines backed down to a tolerable 75 or so as the flaps were withdrawn and by the time we reached cruising altitude, I was well into *Nicholas Nickelby* on my Kindle. In retrospect, I should have been suspicious because of the smoothness of this flight that it was all too good to be true and an hour into our European journey it was announced by one of the flight crew that a warning light had appeared in the cockpit indicating possible malfunction of the horizontal stabilizers. Because we were still closer to Dover AFB than to McGuire AFB in New Jersey (where there were many C5A Galaxies), we were returning to Delaware. We were back on our original, beloved tarmac at 2130 next to the parked C17 we should have used in the first place. Had there been a genuine problem with the horizontal stabilizers and not just the warning light, I would have prayed rather than cursed in silence. When it was announced at 2230 that the warning light system could not be replaced or repaired and the flight scrapped until the same time Saturday, I knew the trip to Leipzig was over. Even worse, I could sense the powerful vacuum-hold Dover had on me. I simply had to get out of this town and get back to my Honda Pilot patiently waiting for me in Charleston. I summoned a cab and asked the driver to take me to the Dover, DL, bus station. I was determined to take any bus going south. Larger cities have actual bus stations. I never imagined that in some cities the size of Dover, the bus station is a Seven-

Eleven store. Friday night in this "bus station" was bustling with all sizes and shapes of humanity in and out for gas, nachos, beef jerky, chips, cigarettes, the Delaware Lottery, and six-packs or singles in a paper bag. The night manager over the angry staccato of rap music in the background informed me that the bus would arrive at 12:15 AM. There being nowhere to sit, I stood astride my suitcase and was thankful to finally hear the familiar roar of the diesel and snorting of the airbrakes of the Greyhound Bus about half-an-hour later. I lugged my heavy bags outside and asked the driver where the bus was headed. I was excited to hear her announce Norfolk, VA, but crestfallen in an instant to learn that I couldn't pay cash for a ticket on that half-empty bus. I had to have purchased the ticket previously on-line. I could sense that Dover vacuum revving up again. To make matters triply worse I was exhausted, I had no hotel room, and there was a biker's convention in town for the weekend and no rooms to be had anywhere in that fair city. I dragged my luggage to a hotel across the busy thoroughfare and threw myself on the mercy of the night manager. Her computer initially indicated a full house, but after a few minutes located a room on the fourth floor for $150 which I took in a heartbeat. Only moments later, she had to turn down a would-be guest who came begging after me.

Awakening early amid Dover's negative pull on my life, in an angry panic I got on-line and booked an airline ticket out of Baltimore to Charleston and a bus ticket out of the Seven Eleven to Baltimore, 120 miles away. When I suddenly realized that the bus would arrive only 30 minutes before the flight, I cancelled that ticket only wasting another hour of my time. The plane was to leave shortly after 2:00PM and it was now 8:30AM. I had the phone number of the very religious cab driver who had driven me to the Seven Eleven last night and called getting his voice mail telling me to have a "blessed day." I indicated I would pay him to drive me out of this infernal city to Baltimore almost whatever the cost. He returned my call about 11:30AM and in fifteen minutes and $200 we were heading there. We arrived at Baltimore International Airport just about the time the plane had pulled away from the gate. One might think that by now I was as frustrated as Jack Lemon and Sandy Dennis in "The Out of Towners" or Steve Martin and John Candy in "Planes, Trains, and Automobiles", but the freedom from my imprisonment in Dover was exhilarating.

The long security lines prior to the next flight to Charleston, the "zoo" of the Hartsfield International connection, and the taxi to the Air Force Base were, by comparison, minor inconveniences in a hellish captivity in the Dover without the white cliffs. My Honda Pilot was as happy to see me as I was to see her and we drove home together in a clear, starry night. Augusta, GA at 2:00AM can be truly beautiful as I found out for a mere $3000.

The Phone and I

John F. Fisher, MD

*Published in *Down in the Dirt Magazine*, September 2023

My relationship with the telephone has always been schizophrenic—love or hate. My earliest recollections were of a single, ebony device whose base was a rounded rectangle with a pyramidal perch for the receiver on a table in the hall. In the days of party lines, when I tried to use it to call a friend, invariably someone else seemed to be on the line nattering with someone in a high- pitched, strident voice incessantly whining about something or someone. This woman's pitiable husband, assuming anyone would marry her, had to be on the verge of murder or suicide to avoid a psychotic break from a life of acoustic trauma.

When private lines, wall phones, and a second one in the bedroom became commonplace, I began to view them as quite convenient for conversations with friends or prospective dates, unless my mother might be listening on the extension. In college, calls were all outgoing on a payphone, collect to my parents, or to a girlfriend until I ran out of quarters which was usually in middle of my alibi as to why I hadn't called lately. My next call to her moments later yielded a busy signal.

Notwithstanding the occasional annoyance, I kept a mostly favorable view of telephones until I became an intern at Cincinnati Children's when the device developed an attitude toward me. After it rang that first night in the on-call quarters I remember thinking that I had an opportunity to show the nurses how nice I could be, despite being startled awake at 2:00AM after just dozing off. I was almost as nice at 3:30AM, but at the 5:00AM call, I was completely faking it. Since my call schedule was every other night for the year, the phone became my adversary, on the rare occasion that I was even able to lie down. Even rarer was the ability to address the nurse's phone request while still supine. For the most part, I was able resist the temptation to slam the receiver down, but it was usually necessary to get out of bed and go to a child's bedside for an exam or to restart an iv. Restarting ivs in infants or toddlers was always challenging because there was no reasoning with the little angels as to why they were needed in the first place and no way to make the butterfly needle less painful. Moreover, these little veins were hard to stick after the several minutes (at least) it took to find one. In babies, a phone call about an infiltrated iv meant at least 30 minutes at the crib-side to change one and there was no waiting until morning because all of them needed the fluids and usually antibiotics too. But taking good care of sick people is what I signed up for. So, quit your whining and complaining, Doctor! Nevertheless, those days and the countless calls in my career which followed explain my Pavlovian aversion to a telephone call to this day.

Nowadays, I have a phone, you have a phone, and most of God's children have a phone--on their person! But the exception is that you *like* yours and your entire world revolves around it. Amazingly, right now, you can and *do check* 10 crucial things like:

1. How the exact Greenwich Mean Time corresponds to that on your Apple watch

2. How the precise temperature correctly has provided an explanation to the sweat staining the underarms of your shirt or blouse

3. Each of the company and private emails you received while you were at lunch or at exercise including the ones about fashion, insurance, and sundry phishing attempts you are receiving now

4. Texts and images from twelve friends and family members describing each of their activities in real time

5. The latest scores from sporting events including Rory McIlroy's score on hole number eight in the second round of the Arnold Palmer Invitational

6. Tweets from the President and his adversaries or by celebrities which call for an immediate favorable or vitriolic response

7. Confirmation from the weather app that it is actually raining now and

how fast that cell is moving

8.   The exact distance or number of steps you have taken to this point today

9.   Your precise GPS location on your neighborhood walk with your dog when you stop to clean up after him

10.   The people who liked or loved the image or video you posted in the last hour on Facebook or Instagram

The beauty of these enterprises is that, if you are skillful, you can do all this while driving or without having to make eye contact with any passerby. True, you may bump into someone on the sidewalk or sideswipe the car next to you as you are looking down, but you are content in your own little world and needn't interact in person with anyone anymore.

I, on the other hand, will be holstering my phone, expecting to hear from no one and, I dare say, hoping for no robocalls about an extended warranty for my car or unwanted texts about hearing aids. Instead, I will be enjoying a ride or walk out in Mother Nature. Furthermore, I will relish the silence of quiet contemplation about my time on this planet with family, friends, and former patients, grateful that I am still alive, hoping I have made a difference to some of these people. I might even pray. While you are checking out the number of likes, loves, and emojis for your most recent post on Facebook, I will be enthusiastically planning to give my next project my full attention today without distraction, hoping that it will be of some benefit to someone— perhaps even you.

Do Turtles Go to Heaven?--Even Elmer?

John F. Fisher, MD

Originally published in *Down in the Dirt Magazine*,
September 2023

I am fully aware that there are turtles who snap when provoked or trying to protect their young, but the image most of us carry with us about a turtle is that of a humble, benevolent, and gentle creature who seemingly immovably sits in the sun with a group of friends on a bank or a rock near a quiet pond. Not infrequently, when out on the back roads in the summer, we encounter a box turtle struggling to cross to the other side, presumably to get to another pond or perhaps to a girlfriend. I hope she is patient, because this process may take hours.

Whenever I see this reptile-crossing-drama unfolding on a country road, my pangs of guilt always recrudesce and I am back in medical school. Probably on a Friday or Saturday night after a grueling week of exams, I had just returned my date for the evening back to the nurses' dorm around midnight. I recall being rather cavalier about the number of beers I had consumed, my driving, and the car I had borrowed from my good friend, Gil, for the evening when I suddenly noticed Elmer. This tortoise was about the size of my fist and he was probably heading home from *his* date for the evening across the road. I had always had a boyhood fascination with these hapless creatures who could never escape being handled by me and my friends for amusement whenever we encountered one. That and my lowered inhibitions from the juice of the barley this evening prevailed on me to pull over to the curb. He was old enough to have had this sort of thing happen before and was likely thinking, "Oh no! Not another car! Don't pull over!

Elmer obviously wasn't happy to see me and closed his hatch when I approached. Indeed, I never did get a look at his face, but I planned to after I got him back to the apartment I shared with my classmate, Pat. Elmer wasn't heavy as I thwarted his trek across the asphalt and altered his life forever. His closed shell fit perfectly in my hand and we got back in the car together. I hesitated to place him on the passenger seat for fear of any untoward emissions which might stain something. However, the empty glove compartment provided a perfect alcove with a door and in went Elmer without any protest for a thrilling ride, faster than any hare he'd ever encountered. I doubt if he even poked his head out until we came to a stop back at Gil's apartment. Unfortunately for Elmer, I didn't think about him on my cab ride home after returning the car. In fact, my memory of this drive-by, turtle-napping had vanished by next morning.

Three weeks later, I got a call from Gil. He had spent the previous 30 minutes trying to discover the origin of the stench emanating from his car in the ninety-degree, summer afternoon of Richmond, Virginia. He had scoured the vehicle both under the seats, in the trunk, and even under the hood for the cause of the fetid odor which pervaded everything and made driving anywhere impossible. This spoor shouldn't have come from the glove box, but it did! There was no 'Rest in Peace' marker for that grave-- the rotten carrion inside of a tortoise shell was all that was left of Elmer.

When Gil inquired if I knew anything about this, my memory along with my guilty conscience rose up volcanically. I was immediately painfully contrite, and Gil, good-natured chum that he is, forgave me. I didn't inquire as to where and how he disposed of Elmer's carcass, but I imagine he was gloved up and held Elmer at arm's length for much of the process. I can still picture what the cardboard walls and floor of his erstwhile prison must have looked like with random, desperate scratch and gouge marks everywhere and the occasional stain or dried turtle chip from an anguished effluent. From the perspective of the SPCA, my villainy deserves a punishment in-kind such as being stuffed in a gym locker in an abandoned high school near Death Valley or rocketed to Mars in a one-way space capsule to fend for myself. A six-figure financial donation to their cause could not begin to assuage my sin.

Elmer's girlfriend is likely still alive after all these years and patiently awaiting his return which has taken a little longer than the few days she customarily expects in these sorts of courtships, but perhaps she has moved on.

Elmer certainly didn't deserve the martyrdom I gave him and, if turtles are allowed in heaven, he went straight there. I, however, should spend at least three weeks in a locked cell in Purgatory inside the shell of a 500-

pound Galapagos tortoise before my release.

The Annual Meeting and the Assistant Professor

John F. Fisher, MD

Last year Patrick O'Shaughnessy, MD, missed the annual fall infectious disease meeting in San Diego where, reportedly, a good time was had by all. Someone on the faculty had to cover the ID service while the others in the division were gallivanting and Pat was most junior and straight out of training in July. He and a third-year resident on the ID elective averaged eight new consults a day while the others were away. After two days of this marathon, the resident found some rather imaginative excuses to get away by five o'clock. Pat was a nice guy and wanted a good reputation with all the house staff, so he didn't object. That left Pat hoping he could get home by eleven. He made it twice during that week.

But this was *this* year and the meeting begins Monday in Boston and the Red Sox are in the World Series. A Hibernophile from childhood, Pat booked a hotel near Faneuel Hall and only a block from *The Black Rose* pub, rumored to be a watering hole for members of the IRA to safely "talk a little treason." The hotel was a walk of about 30 minutes from the Convention Center which, as Granddad O'Shaughnessy would say, "…is just a good stretch of the legs." So on Monday morning, clad in traditional Navy blazer and khaki trousers, he headed jauntily for the meetings. Upon entering the Convention Center, he grabbed a bagel and a large dark-roast from a kiosk and got into a lengthy queue for his badge, abstract brochure, and a canvas logo bag. In front of the line fifteen minutes later, while fumbling to silence the rather odd ringtone on his phone, Pat spilled his coffee on the counter. He blotted up most of it before the drippings could reach the fifth brochure in the nearby stack. Unfortunately, he could do nothing except apologize about the large, brown stain on the yellow blazer uniform of the convention employee. The latter, looking violated, was not especially gracious in his acceptance. Red-faced, Pat franticly scurried to a chair a hundred yards from the registration booths to review the brochure and never ventured near the scene of that crime again.

His interest since fellowship training had been in fungal infections, so he focused on those subjects in locating sessions for the week. Negotiating a confusing maze of meeting rooms and escalators, he eventually found the fungal symposium in an obscure corner of the huge facility. He flashed his ID badge and tip-toed into a lecture on opportunistic infections already in progress. The room was dark and humid, no seats were available, and young people were squatting against the walls half-listening--checking messages, tweets, Instagrams, and Facebook on their cellphones. Pat soon understood this malaise because the speaker, whose celebrated CV listed over 300 peer-reviewed papers, spoke in a strident monotone and read each of the bullets on eighty PowerPoint slides to the audience word for word. The audience's concentration on the lecture was further hampered by the speaker's laser pointer which revealed a distracting intention tremor on the screen and was sometimes absentmindedly directed at their faces.

The restlessness of the audience dying to get out of there was palpable with many furtive glances at wristwatches. Those in front hadn't the courage to get up and leave because the speaker was a world authority on the subject and knew many of them by name. As he droned on, Pat noticed several in the crowd having an embarrassing fight with eyelids that seemed determined to close and heads resolved to nod putting some of them in real danger of a severe whiplash injury. Predictably, this expert's talk was running 15 minutes past his allotted time and he stubbornly scrolled quickly through the last few slides as the moderator approached and finally cut him off by joining him at the podium in mid-sentence and pushing 'B' on the keyboard.

As Day One wore on, Pat noted that the majority of research presentations were also standing-room-only in meeting rooms. Following each speaker there was a lineup at microphones for questions. Some questioners introduced themselves and the medical school they represented and were earnestly seeking clarification of concepts presented. Others began with their surname followed by, "Yale" or "Harvard" or simply "New Haven" or "Boston." Their sole aim was to alert the audience of their presence and importance on the planet. Their questions were lengthy and pedantic which clarified nothing, highlighted their own work, and likely struck terror in a speaker. Tachycardic and sweating profusely, he or she hoped to conjure up a coherent reply without stammering or revealing that they never understood the obtuse question in the first place.

Benefitting marginally at several stereotypical sessions like these, Pat decided to visit the poster sessions and the exhibits. As he expected, there were many posters on *in vitro* and phase II studies of novel antifungals with ID fellows at the ready. He was secretly embarrassed to realize that he had never heard of some of these drugs. It took him stealthily reading and listening to the questions of passersby before he felt comfortable pronouncing drug names like fosmanogepix, ibrexafungerp, and olorofim. By the fourth poster on ibrexafungerp he had grasped enough to haltingly stumble through the pronunciation and ask a timid question about the drug. The fellow's condescending answer indicated that Pat's ruse fooled no one. Humiliated, he decided to head to the exhibits.

There were long lines at the counters of several of the big Pharma booths. He soon discovered that some really desirable items were being given to participants either for completing a 20-minute questionnaire or watching a slick 10-minute video in 3D on the company's product. The most popular item was a laptop-accommodating, backpack duffel bag emblazoned with the familiar corporate logo. Pat finally reached the head of the line for that item and proceeded to fill out the questionnaire. He could tell by some of the questions that his future at the university would likely be interrupted by at least one robocall from the company each week. Nevertheless, he got the backpack and donned it triumphantly. The company certainly got its calculated advertising mileage out of an oblivious Pat wandering about in the huge facility looking for meetings.

The best sessions were late in the afternoon where seats were plentiful and many participants were enjoying an early happy hour or extended lunch in Cambridge and Beacon Hill. While these "scholars" were mildly buzzed and schmoozing with some ID division chiefs, Pat actually got some valuable updates about fungal infections and chatted with one of the world's most respected mycologists. Despite this productive experience, Pat could only give Day One a C-plus and, even on Monday, began to feel that he was a long way from home.

Pondering whether to book a flight home tomorrow, Pat trudged across the Charles River bridge to the hotel, dropped off his duffel bag full of company-funded reprints, exhibit notepads, thumb drives, and novel phone rechargers and headed for *The Black Rose*. He slipped into a booth, ordered a Guinness, and began to imagine himself once again in Ireland. Encouraged by his Granddad, he had taken a two-month elective in pediatrics at the National University as a senior medical student. The Irish music began as his shepherd's pie and another Guinness were served. Pat was in his reverie about Connemara, John Wayne, Maureen O'Hara, and Barry Fitzgerald in *The Quiet Man* when a rather menacing looking fellow of about 50 in a black, Aran sweater with a thick Connaught brogue approached him and asked if he would donate fifty dollars to "the cause." The reputation of the IRA made him afraid for his life if he refused the request, so he obliged the stranger. Saying nothing, the Irishman turned and took his seat at the bar and sat there rather fixedly staring at him. Alarmed, Pat waited until the man entered the restroom, paid the check, and hustled through the dark street back to his hotel. Clearly, he couldn't return to *The Black Rose* and the IRA after that experience.

The next morning the desk clerk handed him an envelope left for him by an unnamed stranger. A note inside read, "Thanks, Paddy, for your generous donation for the homeless on the streets of Galway. You left before I could give you these." Enclosed were two tickets to Game 2 of the World Series the next night. Ashamed of his misjudgment of a stranger, he once again, even more jauntily, struck off for the Convention Center. On the flight home Friday, he gave this meeting an A-plus.